# WHAT REALLY HAPPENED

## Copyright © 2022

What Really Happened © 2022. Pat Fogarty

All rights reserved. This book or parts thereof may not be reproduced in any form, stored in any retrieval system, or transmitted in any form by any means—electronic, mechanical, photocopy, recording, or otherwise—without prior written permission of the publisher and the author; except as provided by United States of America copyright law. For permission requests, write to the publisher at: GranitePublishing@gmail.com: Copyright Coordinator: Susan Grant Granite Publishing: Prescott & Dover. May 2022

ISBN 978-1-950105-38-0
Granite Publishing
Prescott & Dover

9 8 7 6 5 4 3 2
First Edition
Cover Design: Susan Grant

Legal Disclaimer:
This is a work of Creative Nonfiction. No names have been changed; no characters invented. Although the author and publisher have made every effort to ensure that the information in this book is correct, the author and publisher do not assume and hereby disclaim any liability to any party for any loss, damage, or disruption caused by errors or omissions, whether such errors or omissions result from negligence, accident, or any other cause. Sections may include suppositions, opinions of the author, or others and may fall under the guidelines of hearsay and not as indisputable facts. Neither the publisher nor the author shall be responsible for the accuracy of hearsay information. The author and the publisher are aware of the misspellings of names in a few of the archived newspaper articles. And the publisher and author are aware of conflicting addresses and conflicting reports in different articles. The reader should be aware that a hundred years ago many journalists exaggerated the facts to increase the circulation of the particular newspaper they worked for at the time. No citing of any information printed in this book shall be permitted without written permission from the publisher.
Printed in the United States of America

## Table of Contents

| | |
|---|---|
| Table of Contents | v |
| Preface | vii |
| Yellow Journalism | 9 |
| Kidnappings Skyrocket | 47 |
| Gypsies | 106 |
| Final Resting Place | 168 |
| Coroner's Report | 168 |
| Cromwell's Creek | 169 |
| Epilogue | 171 |
| Father Mullin | 172 |
| Detective Joseph Petrosino | 180 |
| Oscar Wilgerodt | 184 |
| What Really Happened | 195 |
| Name Changes | 199 |
| The Author | 201 |

# Preface

I first learned of the 1901 disappearance of Little Willie McCormick when I was a kid in the 1950s. My family lived in the Bronx neighborhood where the young boy had vanished. An elderly man with a disability lived in the same apartment building as my family and he was the first person who told me the story of little Willie's disappearance.

My disabled neighbor had a daughter who would drop off a month's worth of food at the beginning of each month. She lived in the suburbs and she never stayed long.

That left me, his dependable neighbor & errand boy, to shop for the things his daughter never bought for him. A few times a week, I would go to the store for things like pipe tobacco, candy bars, cold cuts, and newspapers. When I returned with his stuff, he always had a story to tell and I had to listen to his stories before he gave me a nickel or a dime for running to the store. Back then, a nickel was a fair tip for a ten-year-old. Five cents would buy a good-sized candy bar or a small coke at the soda fountain.

I never thought much about the stories he told me. But the one about little Willie always made me wonder; *What Really Happened?*

This book contains a collection of newspaper articles from across America that were published and read by the public in 1901. None of the articles were altered. The vernacular of the day, the misspellings, the grammar, and the punctuation used by newspaper reporters of 1901 may seem a bit odd to the modern reader. But, that's just part of the ever-changing English language. Plus; customs and the words used over 120 years ago may seem rude and even offensive to some. That's part of history and I certainly do not want to offend anyone or any organization.

As you work your way through this book, you will most likely notice quite a few investigative actions by the police of 1901 that will make you cringe and wonder how they ever caught any criminals.

On March 27, 1901, ten-year-old Willie McCormick gave his mother a quick hug, put on his favorite wool cap, and waved goodbye as he dashed from his Bronx home to join up with two of his older sisters.

The girls had left moments earlier to start a five-block walk to Sacred Heart Church on Marcher Avenue. It was the Wednesday evening before Palm Sunday and Willie had planned to attend a 7 o'clock benediction. The girls returned home at 8 o'clock and when questioned as to Willie's whereabouts, they told their parents that he never arrived at the church service. Upon hearing the news, Willie's mother became hysterical and fainted.

Mr. McCormick and several neighbors immediately began searching for the boy. Gertrude, Willie's 12-year-old sister, ran to a nearby police station and told the desk sergeant that her brother was missing. The sergeant alerted his men to be on the lookout for the young lad.

By morning, the news of Willie's disappearance appeared in all the local newspapers. By late afternoon, conflicting stories about Willie's fate were being printed. *The New York Times* fallaciously reported that the boy was being held for ransom. *The New York World* claimed to possess reliable information indicating that Willie had run away from home. And, *The New York Sun* ran a column stating that the boy was seen in the company of three gypsies on a train heading to Virginia. These unconfirmed and outright bogus stories sold plenty of newspapers, but they also caused the police to waste valuable time chasing false leads.

The mysterious disappearance of Little Willie McCormick soon became the most ardent and most publicized search for a missing child in American History.

No case of a missing child in the USA would evoke the interest of the public and provoke Newspapers across the USA and the World to comment and dissect every clue in the disappearance of a child until the abduction of the Lindbergh baby on June 1, 1932.

## New York Times March 30, 1901

### A BRONX BOY MISSING.

**Theory Advanced that His Father's Creditor Kidnapped Him.**

The High Bridge police have spent two days scouring the country in that neighborhood for ten-year-old Willie McCormick, son of William McCormick of One Hundred and Sixty-fifth Street and Ogden Avenue, who mysteriously disappeared Wednesday night and has not been seen since. Wednesday night the boy left his home to go to the Church of the Sacred Heart. That is the last time he was seen.

The parents of the boy and their friends believe the lad has been kidnapped and advance the theory that possibly one of the elder McCormick's creditors has kidnapped the boy. Mr. McCormick failed in business recently. The boy is four feet in height, has dark brown hair, blue eyes, and wore a checked suit, tan overcoat, black shoes and stockings, and a cap.

## The New York Tribune March 30, 1901

### POLICE HAVE SCOURED HIGHBRIDGE DISTRICT FOR TWO DAYS FOR THE LAD.

The Highbridge police have spent two days scouring the country in that neighborhood for Willie McCormick, ten years old, son of William McCormick, of One-hundred-and-sixty-fifth-st. and Ogden-ave., who mysteriously disappeared Wednesday night.

The boy's father was for some time a fruit dealer in West One-hundred-and-twenty-fifth-st. Recently he failed, and it is said was arrested. Since that time, it is alleged, he has been a prisoner in Ludlow Street Jail twice. On Wednesday night the boy left his home to go to the Church of the Sacred Heart, of which Father Mullin is the rector. He has not been seen since then.

The parents of the boy and their friends believe the lad has been kidnaped, and advance the theory that possibly one of the elder McCormick's creditors has kidnapped him. The boy is four feet in height, has dark brown hair and blue eyes, and wore a checked suit, tan overcoat, black shoes and stockings and a cap.

## The New York Times March 31, 1901

### NO TRACE OF MISSING BOY.

#### Friends and High Bridge Police Vainly Hunt for Willie McCormick.

No trace has yet been found of ten-year-old Willie McCormick, son of William McCormick of One Hundred and Sixty-fifth Street and Ogden Avenue, who started from his home for the Roman Catholic Church of the Sacred Heart Wednesday evening, and has not been seen since.

Capt. Gannon of the High Bridge Police Station had twelve policemen working on the case yesterday, and had also enlisted the services of about a dozen of the little boy's school friends. A thorough search has been made of the caves and woods in the vicinity. Mr. McCormick clings to the theory that his boy has been kidnapped, and takes a very gloomy view of the situation, being convinced that he will never see him again.

Willie was the only boy in a family of twelve, and the night of his disappearance was the first time in his life that he had ever been out of his house alone in the evening.

## Mr. William McCormick Sr.

*Below you will find a little background information about little Willie's father that may or may not have appeared in any of the news articles in this collection.*

In a suspected kidnapping case, the first people the police question are the parents. The information provided by the parents and other household members is often the key to solving the disappearance of a child.

Besides the immediate family, the neighbors and friends of the family are interviewed to gather all facts about the missing person.

Much of the initial information and future articles appearing in newspapers about the McCormick family were not always true.

For one, Mr. McCormick was not a failed Fruit Dealer on 125th Street as reported by the *New York Tribune* on March 30th.

Mr. McCormick was a successful Flower Wholesaler with three large warehouses near Pier 69 on the Hudson River.

The flower business in 1901 was extremely lucrative. Ships from South America and Europe arrived daily with large supplies of fresh flowers cooled with large slabs of ice mined from ice-bearing mountains in Europe and South America.

Flowers that arrived by ship in New York were unloaded and packed into railroad freight cars and shipped across America.

Mr. McCormick was one of the very wealthy middlemen importing, storing, and shipping the flowers.

However, in 1897 Mr.McCormick borrowed money from several businessmen with the promise of making them partners.

Shortly after Mr. McCormick borrowed the money his 3 warehouses burned to the ground. Mr. McCormick filed for bankruptcy and retired from the wholesale flower business.

Lawsuits from the investors followed. The final outcome was Mr.McCormick's motion for bankruptcy was granted. The men who invested in Mr. McCormick's flower business lost their investment. However, Mr. McCormick did not get off scot-free. He was sentenced to two years in New Yorks's infamous Ludlow Street Jail.

Mr. McCormick was released from jail in January of 1901; just 2 months before Willie disappeared.

NYC's Ludlow Street Jail was a corrupt institution where "White Collar" criminals with money could serve their time with amenities not found in normal prisons.

BILLIARD-ROOM IN LUDLOW STREET JAIL.—[Sketched by Stanley Fox.]

LUDLOW STREET JAIL—THE OFFICE.

INTERIOR OF CELL.

GROCERY STORE.

## The Evening World April 1, 1901

# STRANGE MAN MAY HAVE KIDNAPPED BRONX BOY.

### Willie McCormick Was Twice Accosted by Well-Dressed Individual Who Wanted the Little Fellow to Accompany Him.

On April 1, 1901, this photo appeared in hundreds of Newspapers Across America

## The Evening World April 1, 1901

On two slender clews the police are to-day trying to unravel a kidnapping mystery.

Willie McCormick, the ten-year-old son of William McCormick, a retired florist, started from his home at Ogden avenue and Elmer Place, in the Bronx, on Wednesday night, for church, with his two sisters.

The lad returned in a few minutes for his overcoat. He was helped into it and skipped off to join his sisters. His family have not seen him since.

Harry Russell, one of Willie's companions, told The Evening World to-day that while they were playing together early last week, Willie was accosted by a tall, well-dressed man. The stranger asked to be directed to a certain street. He asked Willie to accompany him, and point out the way, but the lad was suspicious of him and refused. Later the man returned and asked Willie to take a trolley ride. Willie was alarmed and ran away. The boy did not tell his parents of the incident.

Conductor Murray, of a Fifth avenue surface car, in Brooklyn, said to-day that he was positive Willie McCormick had ridden on his car from the Thirty-ninth street ferry to Coney Island on Saturday. He had read the boy's description and could not be mistaken.

The boy's parents scout the idea of their son making a trip to Coney Island or being a fugitive from home.

### *The Evening World April 1, 1901*

> Willie was an only son. He was the baby and enjoyed the care of his parents and eleven sisters. He was naturally a good boy, gentle in manner and rather timid. His father said the lad would not sleep at night unless the door between his room and his mother's were left open.
>
> "I am certain," said Mr. McCormick, "that the boy has been kidnapped. He would not have run away and he was too well acquainted with the country about here to wander to the Harlem River and fall in, as the police suggest. Some one was lying in wait to kidnap him when he went out to church with his sisters. They supposed I had money. I was wealthy once, but I have little left."
>
> The police of the Kingsbridge station say that they are completely puzzled by the lad's disappearance.

## Were Newspapers helping in the search for Little Willie, or were they hindering the police with their unscrupulous reporting?

Newspapers in the early 1900s were the primary source of news for the American public. There were no radios, televisions, or computers at the beginning of the 20th century. And, although Alexander Graham Bell had invented the telephone in 1876, only the rich and powerful had phones in their homes in 1901.

Telegraph service ruled the media world at that time. By the early 1900s, every town across the country with a railroad station usually had a Depot office with a ticket agent who also served as the local telegraph operator.

Long-distance phone calling was not an option. Telephone companies still had a slew of technical problems to overcome before the telephone became a workable reality for sharing news across America.

Savvy newspaper reporters gathered at railroad depots to get the latest national news coming across the telegraph wires. And while they were waiting for breaking stories, they were in the right place to get all the local news and gossip from travelers coming to and leaving town.

In the larger Cities and Towns, most metropolitan Newspaper Offices had a telegraph station and operator on the premises for their reporters to send and receive stories.

## The Sad Truth About Unethical Newspaper Publishers

# Yellow Journalism

The term Yellow Journalism originated with the "Newspaper Wars" during the waning days of the 19th century.

Unfortunately, when Little Willie went missing in 1901 Yellow Journalism was still in its heyday. Lurid and sensational headlines which defined Yellow Journalism had a mesmerizing grip on newspaper publishers and the average reader.

The two largest newspaper owners in America at the time were Joseph Pulitzer and William Randolph Hearst. These two men were fierce and unscrupulous competitors. The newspaper wars between these two publishers and other newspaper barons began in New York City in the 1890s. Exaggerated, racy, and misleading headlines continued to be practiced during the early years of the 20th century.

By 1901 Pulitzer and Hearst had perfected the nefarious art of Yellow Journalism with most of the Independent Newspapers across the country following suit.

Hearst and Pulitzer realized, that the more startling the headline, the more newspapers they sold. Other newspaper publishers across the country, who observed these two media giants gain readership with sensational headlines and wildly exaggerated stories, followed their example by printing outlandish headlines and publishing wildly unsubstantiated stories.

*The Evening World April 2, 1901*

# THREAT TO BURN OUT KIDNAPPED BOY'S EYES

## Ransom Left for Willie McCormick's Kidnappers Not Taken by Men.

The kidnappers of William McCormick have demanded $200 in gold for his ransom. For non-compliance, they threaten to burn out the lad's eyes.

The money has been placed, according to their directions, in an iron pot found, as they intimated, in an old washboiler in a vacant lot at One Hundred and Thirty-fifth street and Third avenue, in the borough of the Bronx.

The letter demanding ransom was received by the boy's father at noon yesterday. He took it to Capt. James Gannon of the Highbridge station. Detectives Brownell and O'Leary found the boiler mentioned in the letter. Then McCormick, by the advice of the police, put the $200 in the place designated.

It is there yet.

### Detectives Watched.

Detectives Browne watched it from night all night. The kidnapped the watched the were aware of the police. Thence. The get the money, money, mean certain arrest in arr

Mr. McCormick Cormick day that he had he ha ing letters demanding money, ter and the postal card in it, were given to The Evening World by the police.

Assured that the McCormick boy was kidnapped and is in durance somewhere within the city the police department is bending every effort to unearth the crime.

In all things the kidnappers of Willie McCormick patterned their actions after those of the Cudahy kidnappers.

### Revenge the Motive.

The police believe that revenge rather than a desire for gain is the motive for the crime.

## *The Boston Globe* April 2, 1901

# Bold Kidnapping From Highbridge, N Y.

## Police Believe That a Lad is Held for Ransom.

They Search Five Days and Nights for Young Willie McCormick—Father Supposes the Captors Have Been Deluded Into the Idea That He is Wealthy, But His Fortune Has Been Swept Away.

NEW YORK, April 2—Willie McCormick, the 10-year-old Highbridge boy who disappeared Wednesday night last, is the victim of a daring kidnapping plot. He is being held for ransom.

The police say that they are certain of this.

For five days and nights the police have been searching the city and its suburbs without finding a trace of the lad. If the earth had opened up and swallowed him up when he came out of his father's house that evening on his way to church his disappearance could not have been more complete.

The case is full of mystery. The police evidently have some ground on which to base their belief that the boy is held for ransom.

Mr McCormick, the father, is at a loss to understand why kidnappers should have seized his boy, as he is not wealthy. He said that reverses had taken the fortune he once possessed. He believed the kidnappers may have been deceived into their desperate undertaking by the fact that his home in Ogdens av, near Elmer pl, is a spacious and attractive one.

The boy's mother has taken to her bed, completely prostrated by the great grief that has come to her. The father, who has remained up night after night, watching every opportunity to get trace of his missing boy, also became exhausted by the great strain, and was forced to seek rest today.

## *The Evening Times* April 2, 1901

### NEW YORK BOY DISAPPEARS.

#### Belief That He Is Being Held by Kidnappers for Ransom.

NEW YORK, April 1.—The mother of ten-year-old Willie McCormick, jr., is prostrated at her home this morning and it is positive that her boy has been kidnapped.

Willie is the only boy in a family of twelve children and lived with his parents at Ogden Avenue, near Elmer Place. He disappeared on Wednesday evening under such mysterious circumstances as to leave but little doubt that he has been kidnapped.

Two of his sisters asked him to go to church with them and he started out, but ran back for his overcoat. He then started to run after his sisters and since then has not been seen. It is thought that somebody was lying in wait to kidnap him.

William McCormick, the boy's father, is a retired florist and was once quite wealthy. He believes the boy is being held for ransom.

## *Boston Globe* April 2, 1901

### GLOBE EXTRA! 5 O'CLOCK

### BOY STOLEN.

### Bold Kidnapping From Highbridge, N.Y.

### Police Believe That a Lad is Held for Ransom.

They Search Five Days and Nights for Young Willie McCormick—Father Supposes the Captors Have Been Deluded Into the Idea That He is Wealthy, But His Fortune Has Been Swept Away.

## The Arrow indicates the location of Sacred Heart Church

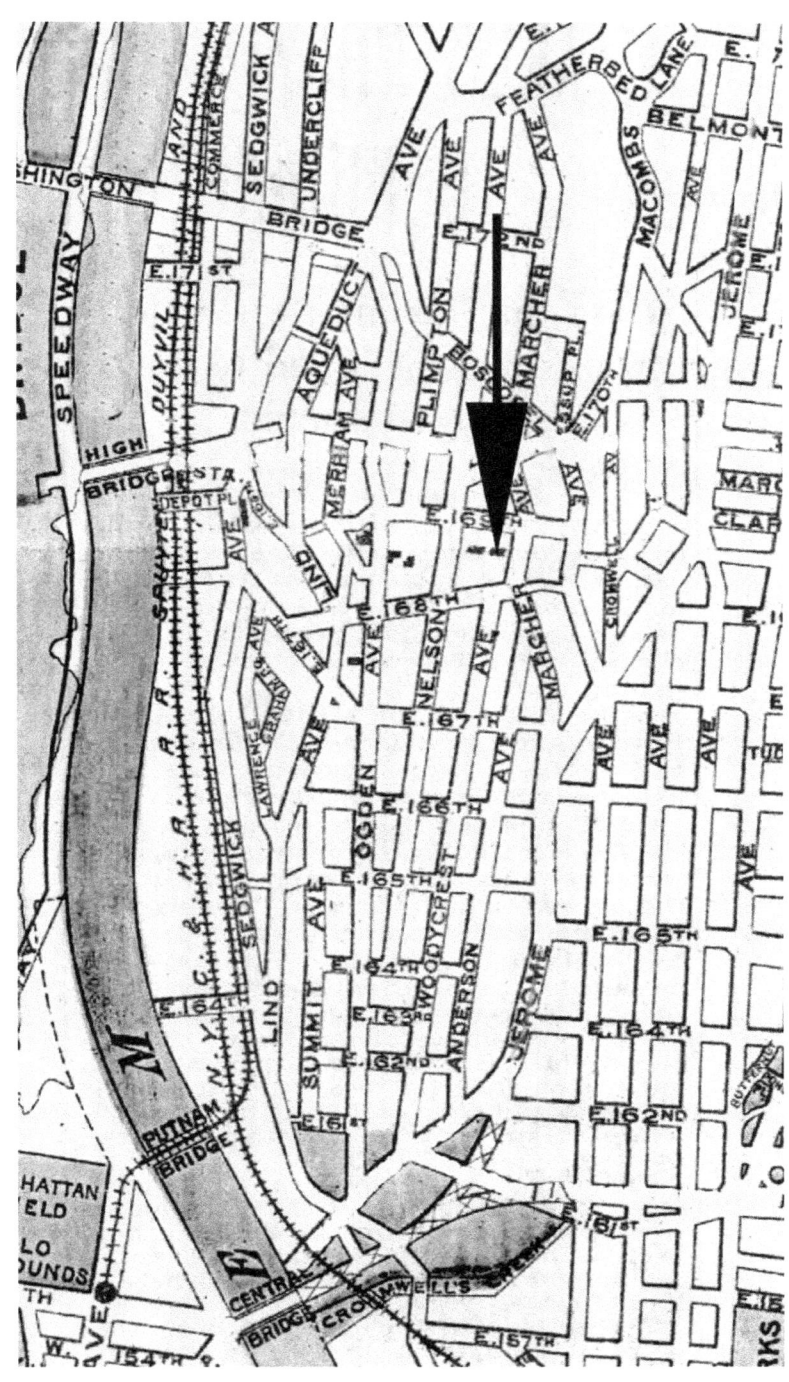

## *Buffalo Evening News April 2, 1901*

# FALLS PREY TO KIDNAPERS.

## Willie McCormick of Highbridge Now Believed to Have Been Abducted.

(By Associated Press.)

NEW YORK, April 2.—After vainly running out every clue the police became convinced last night that Willie McCormick, Jr., a 10-year-old Highbridge boy, who disappeared last Wednesday night, was the victim of a kidnaping plot.

Capt. Titus of the Central Detective Bureau and Capt. James Gannon of the Highbridge Police Station have put every available man on the case.

On Wednesday night two of the boy's sisters were going to church with him when he found it necessary to return to the house for his overcoat. He was delayed for a few moments, and the sisters walked toward the church. When he failed to rejoin them soon they walked rapidly to the church, both believing until they had returned home that he had decided not to go with them. As a matter of fact he had slipped on his overcoat and started after them.

Capt. Gannon, in discussing the case, said:

"This boy was never known to be away from home over night. His habits were good, and there had been nothing to drive him away from home. I am of the opinion that he is being held here in New York City."

The child has 11 sisters. His mother is prostrated from grief and anxiety, and the father, who is a retired florist, almost equally so.

## *The Boston Globe April 2, 1901*

# Bold Kidnapping From Highbridge, N.Y.

## Police Believe That a Lad is Held for Ransom.

**They Search Five Days and Nights for Young Willie McCormick—Father Supposes the Captors Have Been Deluded Into the Idea That He is Wealthy, But His Fortune Has Been Swept Away.**

NEW YORK, April 2—Willie McCormick, the 10-year-old Highbridge boy who disappeared Wednesday night last, is the victim of a daring kidnapping plot. He is being held for ransom.

The police say that they are certain of this.

For five days and nights the police have been searching the city and its suburbs without finding a trace of the lad. If the earth had opened up and swallowed him up when he came out of his father's house that evening on his way to church his disappearance could not have been more complete.

The case is full of mystery. The police evidently have some ground on which to base their belief that the boy is held for ransom.

Mr McCormick, the father, is at a loss to understand why kidnappers should have seized his boy, as he is not wealthy. He said that reverses had taken the fortune he once possessed. He believed the kidnappers may have been deceived into their desperate undertaking by the fact that his home in Ogdens av, near Elmer pl, is a spacious and attractive one.

The boy's mother has taken to her bed, completely prostrated by the great grief that has come to her. The father, who has remained up night after night, watching every opportunity to get trace of his missing boy, also became exhausted by the great strain, and was forced to seek rest today.

## Boston Globe—cont'

There are 11 daughters. All share with their parents the great grief of losing the only son in the family. It is with difficulty that they retain their composure, and many times their eyes fill with tears as they tell over again the circumstances under which Willie disappeared.

Every member of the McCormick family adheres to the belief, formed the day after the boy had disappeared, that he has been made the victim of a cruel plot.

Capt Titus of the police detective bureau and Capt Gannon of Highbridge have scores of detectives working on the case.

Capt Gannon said today: "We are now working upon a clew which, I believe, will result in finding the missing boy. The kidnappers may have taken the boy on a train passing Highbridge in the dead of night. He may now be miles from here.

Capt Gannon added that every section of the city and all points adjacent to the metropolis had been scoured during the last three or four days and nights, and that this work would be continued unceasingly until the missing boy was found.

There are rumors that threats have been made to the family of Mr McCormick, and several of the daughters spoke about this today.

Capt Gannon with detectives John Ryan, Thomas Lamb and Hector Worden, several central office men and policemen Andrew Bruner and David F. Ryan, searched Jessup's woods. They hunted among the trees, waded the creeks and lost no opportunity to find a clew to the absent son.

Mr McCormick has received a letter stating that his boy is in durance, but will be returned unharmed if $200 in gold is left at a certain point in Harlem.

*New York Times April 3, 1901*

# MISSING BOY SEEN ON A BAY RIDGE CAR

## Conductor Recognizes Willie McCormick's Photograph.

### Father Receives Message from "Kidnapper," and Police Watch Ransom Deposited at Place Indicated.

Capt. Gannon of the High Bridge Police Station admitted last night that he and his detectives had come to the conclusion that ten-year-old William McCormick, Jr., who disappeared from his home in Ogden Avenue March 27, had been kidnapped. At the same time, however, Capt. Titus, at Police Headquarters, announced that Detective O'Connell of his staff, had been informed by John Murray, a conductor on the Bay Ridge trolley line, that a boy answering the lad's description had boarded his car on Thursday morning.

Murray readily identified the boy from a photograph. He said that McCormick got on the car at 11:15 o'clock, at Thirty-ninth Street, Brooklyn, and rode to Fifth Avenue and Eightieth Street. Other passengers left the car, and Murray said he had a talk with the little fellow, who said that his father was a gardener living at Eighth Avenue and One Hundred and Thirty-third Street. He said that he had spent the preceding night close to Buffalo Bill's camp at Ambrose Park, and had left because another boy was shot in the eye by a stray bullet. He said that he was going where there were more horses, and Murray thinks he meant to go to the Coney Island race tracks.

## NYT_con't

A watchman at Ambrose Park confirmed the story of the other boy being shot, but was unable to give further particulars, and the police tried without avail to locate the wounded lad, hoping to gain information from him.

Mr. McCormick, the boy's father, on Monday received a letter and a postal card, which have greatly increased his fears. Both were clumsily written, and the letter read as follows:

New York City, March 31, 1901.

Dear Mr. McCormick: I have kidnapped your William. Now, I want you to get $200 in gold and put the money in a red cloth and then tie it up and put the little packet in a square pail at the northeast corner of Third Avenue and One Hundred and Thirty-fifth Street. Don't tell the police. If you do, we will burn the boy's eye out, and if you put the money there and don't tell the police you will have your boy in thirty-eight hours, and if you refuse our order we will burn the boy's eye out and burn him to death. Yours truly, KIDNAPPER.

The postal card came by the same mail and was in the same writing. It read:

April 1, 1901.

Dear Sir: I forgot in the letter to tell you when to come at Third Avenue and One Hundred and Thirty-fifth Street. The square pail is in the large boiler in the northeast corner, and do not come before 8 o'clock to-night. Yours truly, "KID."

The communications, which had been mailed through Postal Station R, at Third Avenue and One Hundred and Fiftieth Street, were turned over to the police, who pronounced them to be the work of some heartless April fool joker. Capt. Gannon attached so much importance to them, however, that he caused Detectives Brownell and Olnan to take $200 in gold to the spot indicated, where they found the square pail. They put the money in it and set a watch for many hours, but no one came near the place.

Up to 2 o'clock this morning no word of the missing boy had been received at his home. A neighbor, Oscar Wullgerodt, has offered $1,000 reward for any clue that will lead to the boy's recovery.

## *April 3, 1901, Marked the First Week of Willie's Disappearance*

False tips, fake ransom notes, and misleading stories printed in newspapers sabotaged the police investigation of the missing child.

However, even with the limited crime-fighting tools law enforcement agencies had at their disposal in 1901, the Highbridge Police did their best to follow up on every clue.

A few weeks before Little Willie McCormick vanished, Police Commissioner Murphy, who considered himself the most anti-corruption Police Commissioner ever appointed to the position, promoted his protegee James Gannor from Sargent to Captain.

James Gannon had come up through the ranks during a very corrupt period of New York Police History. He had the reputation of being a very tough cop and an honest one. Because it was common knowledge that Gannon could not be bribed, he excelled at busting up prostitution rings and illegal gambling houses.

It was also widely known that Commissioner Murphy and the newly appointed Captain Gannon were good friends.

With more than a dozen years of experience fighting crime in some of the toughest parts of New York City, Gannon's reputation for arresting politicians and corrupt Judges made him an outcast amongst the corrupt cops he had to work with.

Yet, even his political enemies and the men and women he arrested were often left wondering: *'How did he manage to always stay one step ahead of them?'*

Muckraking newspaper reporters often printed rumors of his secret sources of information. Brothel owners and the rough characters who ran illegal gambling dens were convinced that Gannon had more than 100 low-level criminals working as informers.

The press and most New York City officials were not surprised when on January 1, 1901, Police Commissioner Murphy announced the promotion of his friend James Gannon from Sargent to Captain. However, it was shocking news when it was announced that Captain Gannon's first command would be the Highbridge Precinct in the Bronx.

In 1901, if a policeman or a higher ranking officer got sent to the Bronx Highbridge Precinct, it usually meant they had screwed up and were being punished.

There were no brothels or gambling joints to be raided in Highbridge. The neighborhood possessed a semi-rural landscape with mostly single-family homes with slate sidewalks and macadamize roads with no street lights.

Plus, there were no fancy restaurants, theaters, all-night drinking establishments, or any of the other amenities a crooked cop could exploit in the Bronx neighborhood.

Highbridge was mostly a very quiet neighborhood in an ethnically diverse square mile of the Bronx where everyone knew their neighbors and their neighbors' children.

Another drawback for a policeman who received a transfer notice sending them to the Bronx was the transit situation. Unlike most Police Precincts in Manhattan and Brooklyn, public transportation to the Bronx was limited.

However, the beginning of the 20th Century was a time when City Politicians had great plans for the Bronx. Several train lines were in the planning stage and there were dozens of Trolly Car Companies seeking permits to build overhead power lines for lucrative contracts in the more developed parts of the Bronx.

With the overcrowded tenements of New York City's lower east side and the need for adequate housing for the ever-growing immigrant population of New York City, large Real Estate firms and builders were beginning to develop the Highbridge area. Vacant lots were being bought and sold by land speculators and small multiple-family homes were starting to sprout up in Highbridge and other parts of the Bronx.

With the massive influx of immigrants living in overcrowded tenements in Manhattan, a building boom for housing sprouted in the outer boroughs of NYC.

*The Buffalo Enquirer April 3, 1901*

## NEW YORK.

# BOY MAY HAVE BECOME A JOCKEY

## Latest Theory Regarding the Mysterious Disappearance of Willie McCormick.

[SPECIAL TELEGRAM TO THE ENQUIRER.]

New York, April 3.—William McCormick, the 10-year-old boy who disappeared last Wednesday, is still missing. The police today have a new theory. It is thought the lad ran away to become a jockey.

The theory is based on the story of a trolley car conductor of Brooklyn that he carried to the race track a boy resembling young McCormick.

Oscar Wilgerodt, a wealthy neighbor of the McCormick family, has offered $1,000 for the safe return of the boy. The pleadings of Wilgerodt's son, a playmate of the missing boy, prompted the generous offer.

## The Montgomery Adviser April 3, 1901

### A BOY IS KIDNAPPED.

**Willie McCormick Believed to Have Been Victim of Plot.**

New York, April 2.—After vainly running out every clew, the police are convinced that Willie McCormick, Jr., a 10-year-old Highbridge boy, who disappeared last Wednesday, is the victim of a kidnapping plot.

Wednesday night two of the boy's sisters were going to church with him, when he found it necessary to return to the house for his overcoat. He was delayed for a few moments, and his sisters walked toward the church. When he failed to rejoin them soon, they walked rapidly to the church, both believeing until they had returned that he had decided not to go with them. As a matter of fact he had slipped on his overcoat and started after them.

Police Captain Gannon, in discussing the case, said: "I am firmly convinced that the boy has been taken by designing persons and is being held by them.

"This boy was never known to be away from home over night. His habits were good, and there has been nothing to drive him away from home. I am of the opinion that he is being held here in New York."

Captain Gannon added that every section of the city and all points adjacent to it had ben scoured during the last three or four days and nights, and this would be continued. The boy is the son of a retired florist living in Ogden Avenue, Highbridge. The child has eleven sisters. His father and mother are prostrated with grief.

## The Arrow indicates the location of the McCormick Home

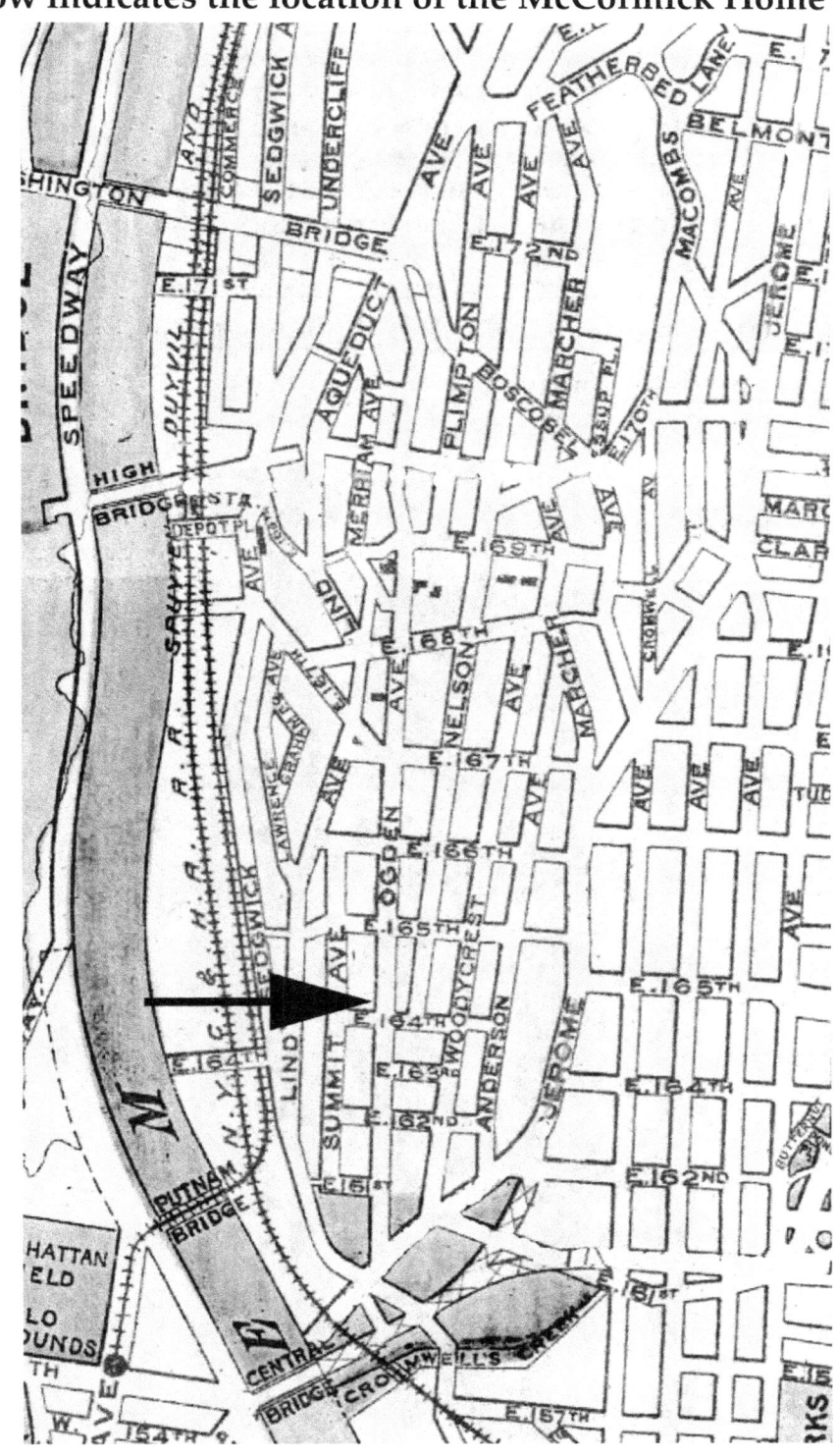

## The Courier News  April 3, 1901

**Reward For Willie McCormick.**

New York, April 3.—Oscar Willgerodt, a wealthy cloak manufacturer, whose boy was a playmate of Willie McCormick, has offered $1,000 reward for the safe return of the missing boy.

On April 3, 1901, this image of Little Willie was published in hundreds of newspapers across America.

WILLIE M'CORMICK.

## The Nashville Banner April 4, 1901

# KIDNAPED WHILE GOING TO CHURCH.

## Mysterious Disappearance of 10-Year-Old Willie McCormick, Jr., Cannot Be Explained in Any Other Way.

New York, April 2.—After vainly running out every clue, the police are convinced that Willie McCormick, Jr., a 10-year-old High Bridge boy, who disappeared last Wednesday, is the victim of a kidnaping plot. Wednesday night two of the boy's sisters were going to church with him, when he found it necessary to return to the house for his overcoat. He was delayed for a few moments, and the sisters walked toward the church. When he failed to rejoin them soon they walked rapidly to the church, both believing until they had returned that he had decided not to go with them. As a matter of fact, he had slipped on his overcoat and started after them.

Police Capt. Gannon, in discussing the case, said:

"I am firmly convinced that the boy has been taken by designing persons, and is being held by them.

"This boy was never known to be away from home over night. His habits were good, and there had been nothing to drive him away from home. I am of the opinion that he is being held here in New York City."

Capt. Gannon added that every section of the city and all points adjacent to it had been scoured during the last three or four days and nights, and that this would be continued. The boy is the son of a retired florist, living in Ogden avenue, High Bridge. The child has eleven sisters. His father and mother are prostrated with grief.

**The tip of the arrow shows the location of Sacred Heart Church.**
Father Mullins lived behind the church, which is indicated by the small rectangle to the left of the arrow point.

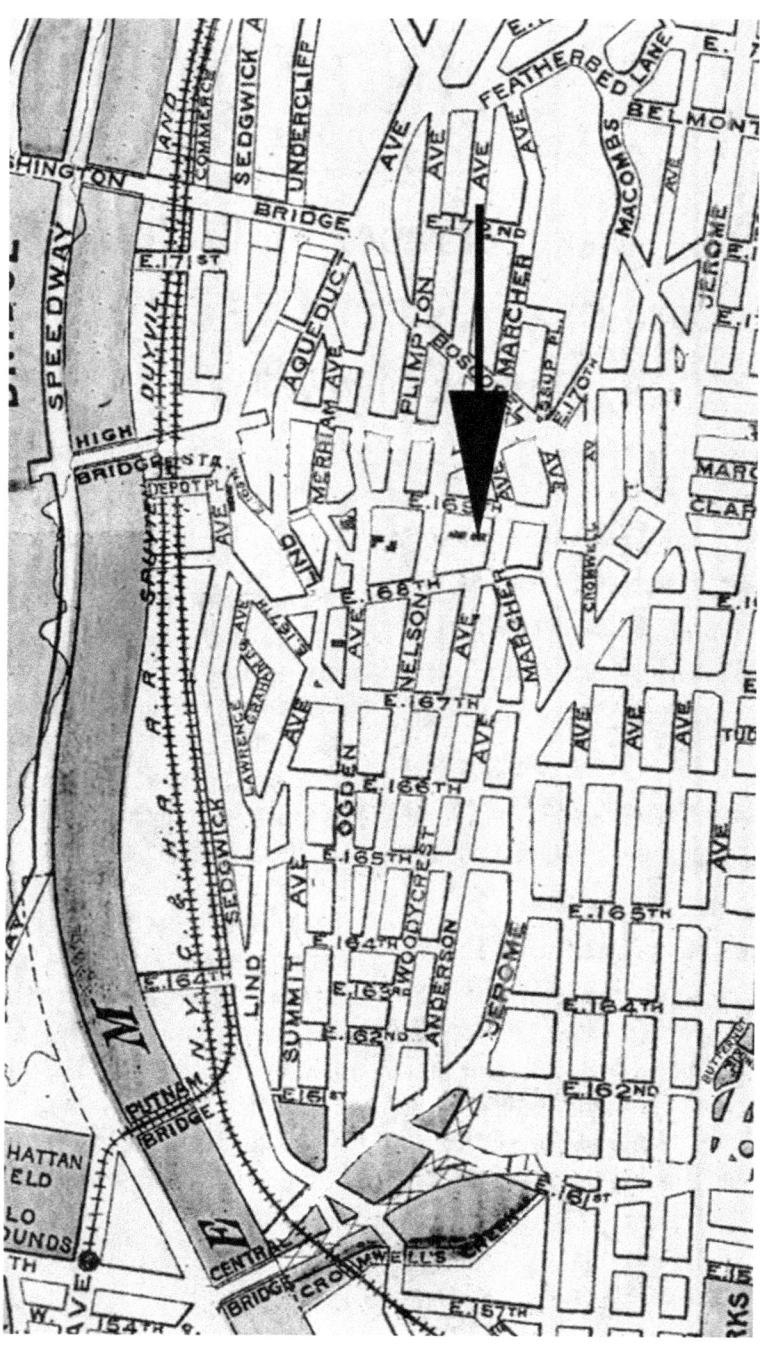

## The New York Sun April 4, 1901

**But Full Investigation Leads the Police to Believe That He's Just a Runaway.**

Willie McCormick, the ten-year-old boy who disappeared from his home in High Bridge a week ago, has not yet been found, but the police have now entirely abandoned the notion that he was kidnapped.

Capt. Titus of the Detective Bureau said yesterday that he regarded the sending of the letter demanding $200 ransom for the boy as merely a cruel hoax. If he could catch the perpetrator, the captain said, he'd make it warm for him. To Capt. Titus's mind Willie's is a plain case of a runaway boy, whose mind had been inflamed by the stories he had heard about Buffalo Bill shows and other sights attractive to boys of his age. Capt. Gannon of the High Bridge station, after paying a visit to Police Headquarters, said that his view of the case, too, was that Willie McCormick had run away.

The police put a great deal of faith in the story of Conductor Murra of the Bay Ridge trolley line, who says that a boy answering Willie's description rode on his car from Thirty-ninth street to Eightieth street, Brooklyn, last Thursday. The description, they say, fits Willie, even to the freckles on his face and other details. The only reason why his family wont believe that the boy the conductor talked with was Willie seems to be their unwillingness on general principles to believe that Willie was the kind of boy to run away. Capt. Titus however learned from one of his men yesterday that Father Mullen of the church Willie attended had found several of Willie's boy friends who declared that ever since he heard of the Buffalo Bill show he had been debating whether to run away or not, his decision seeming to rest on the chance he would have of seeing the horses and the red Indians.

Capt. Titus had detectives hunting around the stables at Sheepshead Bay yesterday with four of Willie's playmates, but they didn't find Willie. To-day they will renew the search.

## New York Sun April 4, 1901

The McCormicks said last night that they had received in the last mail three letters, which they had turned over to the detectives. One, they said, was an anonymous letter. In it the writer said that Willie had been seen in front of the Pulitzer Building walking rapidly toward the Brooklyn Bridge and that a tall man was "walking nervously" behind him.

The others were both threatening letters, the McCormicks said. They would not say anything more about these letters on the ground that the detectives had told them not to. All three of the letters had been mailed at Station R, which is at High Bridge. The McCormicks, according to the police, have been getting letters before this from creditors of Mr. McCormick, who recently went through bankruptcy proceedings. It was intimated by the family that two of last night's letters were from the same source and that the police had taken them thinking they might contain a clue.

## The Brooklyn Citizen April 4, 1901

### MOTHER WAITING FOR WILLIE.

#### Mrs. McCormick Believes that the Little Fellow Will Soon Be Found.

Mrs. McCormick, mother of missing Willie McCormick, put a light in the window, and sat up all night waiting for her boy to return. She has a premonition that he will return soon and wishes to be the first to welcome him.

The police, who have been working industriously on the mystery, say they will find the boy before night. Captain Gannon would not divulge the basis on which this claim is founded.

Another letter written by the alleged kidnappers, was received by the McCormick family last night. It stated that by the time the letter was received the boy would be at sea with his kidnappers.

## *The New York Times* April 4, 1901

## Their Rich Neighbor, Mr. Willgerodt, Explains His $1,000 Reward.

## HABITS OF THE MISSING BOY

### Police Believe Little Willie McCormick Ran Away—More Threatening Letters—Mr. McCormick's Troubles.

Whether little Willie McCormick of High Bridge was kidnapped or not, his father, mother, and many of the neighbors are firmly convinced that he was. Mrs. McCormick was hopeful up to yesterday morning that her little son would be found, but in the afternoon her daughters say she gave up hope, and last night she was completely prostrated.

William McCormick, the father of the missing child, was in a state of collapse last night, also. In fact, the condition of both Mr. and Mrs. McCormick was such that they were unable to see Oscar E. F. Willgerodt, who has offered a reward of $1,000 for the return of the boy, and who called at the house to express his sympathy with the family.

This reward is unique. Mr. Willgerodt, who offers it, is a German and a wealthy cloak merchant. He has a beautiful home on Ogden Avenue, Borough of the Bronx, just overlooking Central Bridge. Mr. Willgerodt lives just down the hill from the McCormick family, but he has never become acquainted with any of its members except two of the older daughters. He has two young children himself, one of them being ten years old and just about the age of little Willie McCormick.

*New York Times cont'*

"We have not an enemy in the world, so far as we know," said Miss McCormick. "We have sent word to every one of our relatives who knew Willie, and we have given the police the names of almost everybody who has ever had any relations with us. We have told them the names of all our servants of the past few years, and have even given them the names of father's creditors. We do not suspect any of these, but the police wanted something, and we gave them these."

William McCormick has been involved in considerable financial difficulty recently, his troubles resulting in his remaining in Ludlow Street Jail for some time. Last Summer he was involved in bankruptcy proceedings. It was suggested that perhaps these facts might have furnished a motive for a kidnapping, where the fact that the father was a poor old man would not suffice. This was why the names of the creditors were furnished to the police.

Miss McCormick said she had made inquiry among all the neighbors to ascertain if they were acquainted with any wildness on his part with which the family was not familiar. She said that every report of the boy was as good as could be. She said she was perfectly willing for the child's record to be investigated in every particular.

### BOY FRIENDS EXCITED.

The small boys of the neighborhood, the playmates of little McCormick, are greatly excited over the disappearance of their friend. They say he was a very good boy, and they believe he was kidnapped without doubt. These boys have learned that reporters and detectives are trying to find out the habits of the McCormick child, and they talk very readily. Their reports have not, however, been of any practical assistance in clearing up the mystery.

## *New York Times cont'*

The boys all agree that Willie McCormick was greatly interested in Buffalo Bill and the Wild West Show. The theory has been advanced that the McCormick child went to Ambrose Park last week, where Col. Cody's rough riders were rehearsing. One story said that he had been frightened away by a chance shot which wounded an acquaintance, and that he had sought the less strenuous excitement of the Sheepshead Bay race track.

Capt. Titus said last night that Father Mullen, who was one of little Willie's preceptors at church, had told him that some of McCormick's playmates had informed the priest that the child had expressed an intention of running away from home and following the Wild West Show.

Miss Marcella McCormick said all such ideas were absurd. She said the boy was idolized by his sisters, of whom there are eleven. She said he had never expressed any great interest in Col. Cody's enterprises, and that he could have had no motive for leaving his own home.

On the other hand, Sergt. Boehm of the High Bridge Station told a NEW YORK TIMES reporter last night that Policeman Tighe, who patrols the "beat" including the McCormick home, had stated to him that Willie McCormick's father had often asked him late at night if he had seen the boy anywhere on the streets. Patrolman Tighe felt that the case was one of runaway, and the other policemen of the neighborhood express the same opinion.

Capt. Gannon of the High Bridge Station was very active in the McCormick case yesterday, although he expressed the belief that the boy had merely run away from home. He spent considerable time at Police Headquarters discussing the case with Capt. Titus and Deputy Commissioner Devery. Capt. Gannon has expressed a number of theories concerning this case, he at one time having stated that he thought it was a kidnapping. He said yesterday:

## New York Times cont'

"Why don't the family tell all they know about this case? They are keeping back things. Now, there has been $6 missing from the house ever since the boy ran away. He took that to have a good time with—it was lying loose on the dining-room table."

The letters the McCormicks received Tuesday threatening dire penalties upon the child if a ransom of $200 in gold was not forthcoming, were regarded yesterday as a cruel hoax. The hoax succeeded in hastening the prostration of Mrs. McCormick. One of these letters had directed Mr. McCormick to leave the money at a certain point at Third Avenue and One Hundred and Thirty-fifth Street.

A decoy package was placed by the police at the spot specified, and detectives were then stationed to watch the place all night. No one appeared.

### MORE THREATENING LETTERS.

Three more letters bearing on the case were received by the McCormick family yesterday. These letters were not given out by the police, to whom they were delivered last night. Miss Marcella McCormick said this of them:

"The first of these letters said that the writer saw Willie in front of The World office on Park Row about 10 o'clock Saturday morning. He was nervous, according to this informant, and was walking rapidly, followed by a well-dressed, apparently very much agitated man. The description given of the boy tallies very accurately with what Willie looked like. The letter was not signed. It was mailed at Station R, the same one in whose district our home is.

"The other two letters were in the same handwriting as the two we received on Tuesday. They made threats similar to

## *New York Times cont'*

those contained in those letters and demanded that certain conditions be complied with. They were mailed at Station R also."

At the High Bridge Station last night it was said that no letters had been given to Capt. Gannon. At Police Headquarters the Sergeant on duty at the desk said that he could not say what detectives called at the McCormick house, but that no new letters had been reported to him.

Miss Marcella McCormick said she had no faith in the reality of the identification by John Murray, a conductor on the Bay Ridge trolley line, who said that he had seen a boy answering the description of the missing boy on his car last Thursday morning. Capt. Titus said, however, that he had investigated Murray's record and that he found the man to be worthy of all confidence. He said he felt convinced from what the man said that the boy had gone from Ambrose Park to Sheepshead Bay.

Capt. Titus sent a number of detectives to Coney Island and Sheepshead yesterday morning to look for the missing boy. The detectives took with them four of McCormick's playmates to assist in the search and possible identification. Capt. Titus said last night that owing to the rain and storm very few children were out playing, and that his men had no success in gaining any new information.

Two detectives attached to the High Bridge Station, Brownell and Ward, were at work looking for the missing child all day yesterday, but up to a late hour last night no developments had been reported by them. Capt. Gannon said last night, after leaving Police Headquarters, that young McCormick certainly had not been kidnapped. He said he expected that by midnight his detectives would be able to tell where the boy was, and that he would be home soon afterward.

## *New York Times* April 4, 1901

### MR. WILLGERODT'S SYMPATHY.

Mr. Willgerodt, without any consultation with members of the McCormick family or any one else so far as reported, went to the High Bridge Police Station Tuesday night and told the Sergeant of the offer he desired to have recorded. The cloak merchant said at his home last night to a NEW YORK TIMES reporter:

"It is a terrible thing that a child should be kidnapped. I firmly believe this little fellow was kidnapped, for I have asked my little boy—who knows him—and some servants of mine who have seen something of the child, about him, and every report that I hear is a good one. I do not believe he ran away, for he was well treated at home. His family are nice people, and I don't believe there are any nicer girls anywhere than Mr. McCormick's daughters.

"Certain it is that the child is missing. Certain it is, also, that the mother and father are broken-hearted over it. When I learned how distressing the situation was, I felt impelled to do something. I will pay the reward of $1,000 very cheerfully if the boy is returned to his parents. I know how I would feel if my child was kidnapped. I do not believe, however, that this child will ever be found."

Mr. Willgerodt said the reports that he had feared his own child would be kidnapped were all false. He also scouted the idea that the McCormick child might have been taken by mistake for his son Oscar. He said the children were too much unlike in every particular for that. Mr. Willgerodt called at the McCormick home last night and expressed his anxiety to do everything in his power to secure the missing child.

Miss Marcella McCormick, the oldest daughter and the active head of the house in these trying times, told Mr. Willgerodt that her father and mother were very grateful to him for his assistance. She said, however, that they were all just as much at sea then as they had ever been, and that while they were sure the child had been kidnapped, they could not formulate the slightest idea as to who might have done the deed.

# Oscar Willgerodt

**In today's world: Investigators would surely have taken a closer look at Oscar Willgerodt.**

Who was Oscar Willgerodt and why would he be the first to offer a reward for the missing boy?

If someone not related to a missing person offered a substantial reward in today's world, the first thing the Police would do is to look into that person's background. And, no matter what they found or did not find, authorities would certainly question the motive of the person offering the reward. Plus, they would check the person's financial standing to see if he or she had the funds to pay the reward.

A Thousand Dollar reward in 1901 was a substantial amount of money for a neighbor to offer for a missing child.

$1,000 in 1901 is equivalent in purchasing power to about $35,500 today, an increase of $34,500 over the years. The dollar had an average inflation rate of 2.92% per year between 1901 and today, producing a cumulative price increase of 3,156.75%

U.S. Federal records show Oscar Willgerodt as a 47-year-old Cloak Merchant living in the Highbridge section of the Bronx in 1900.

At the time of Willie McCormick's disappearance, Oscar was married to a woman named Bertha who was 20 years younger than him. In 1901 Oscar and Bertha were the parents of two young boys. The Willgerodt family lived less than 3 blocks from the McCormick household.

## *Information from the 1900 Federal Census*

Name:           Oscar Willgerodt
Age:            47
Birth Date:     May 1853
Birthplace:     Germany
Home in 1900:   Bronx, New York
Street:         Ogden Avenue
House Number:   150 (917)
Race:           White
Gender:         Male

Immigration Year: 1872
Relation to Head of House: Head
Marital Status: Married
Spouse's Name: Bertha Willgerodt
Marriage Year: 1892
Years Married: 8
Father's Birthplace: Germany
Mother's Birthplace: Germany

Years in USA: 25

Naturalization: Naturalized
Occupation: Cloak Merchant
Months Not Employed: 0
Can Read: Yes
Can Write: Yes
Can Speak English: Yes
House Owned or Rented: Own
Home Free or Mortgaged: F
Farm or House: H

| Household Members | Age | Relationship |
|---|---|---|
| Oscar Willgerodt | 47 | Head |
| Bertha Willgerodt | 27 | Wife |
| Oscar Willgerodt Jr | 7 | Son |
| Hugo Willgerodt | 1 | Son |
| Malwine Georgi | 18 | Servant (Chambermaid) |
| Annie Greenhagen | 27 | Servant (Cook) |
| John Reichenberger | 24 | Servant (Coachman) |
| Frederick Elener | 19 | Servant (Gardener) |

**The Arrow indicates the home of Oscar Willgerodt**

*Buffalo Evening News April 5, 1901*

# BOY WAS NOT KIDNAPED.

## Willie McCormick Said to Have Left Home Voluntarily, and is on His Way Back.

(By Associated Press.)

NEW YORK, April 5.—Captain Gannon of the High Bridge police station, dictated a statement for publication last night in which he certified that Willie McCormick, who had been missing from home for several days, has not been kidnaped, but left home on his own accord.

The captain declares the letters demanding a ransom were fakes, and gave out a letter he received from John S. Wolf, a lawyer of Albany, which says that on Sunday morning, March 30, four tramps and a boy walked from Troy to East Albany, and that in a conversation with a flagman in a shanty at Bath-on-the-Hudson one of the tramps said they were from Harlem. He said they got into a boxcar there to go to Yonkers, but the door was fastened and they were brought to Troy before they could get out.

Mr. Wolf says the boy answered the descriptions of the McCormick boy. The tramp also told the flagmen they were going to catch the first freight train and try to get back to Harlem. Captain Gannon added that he was satisfied the boy was on his way home now.

*St. Louis Dispatch April 5, 1901*

# $1000 REWARD FOR MISSING BOY

## Was He Kidnaped or Did He Run Away?

## THEORIES IN M'CORMICK CASE

## CHIEF OF NEW YORK DETECTIVES SAYS HE WAS NOT STOLEN.

### Claims That the Lad Was Bad, and That He Has Been Seen Since He Left Home, Six Days Ago.

Special to the Post-Dispatch.

NEW YORK, April 5.—Willie McCormick has now been missing from his home in Ogden avenue, Highbridge, for six days. Police, detectives, his family and 50 schoolboys have searched the city for him. Not a trace has been found.

The police accept the story that he has been kidnapperd. "One thousand dollars reward and no questions asked," is the offer of Oscar Wallgardt, a wealthy cloak manufacturer, for the boy's safe return.

Mr. Willgardt is a neighbor of the McCormicks and his boy, Oscar, and little Willie McCormick were playmates.

The threatening letters of the kidnapers demanding $200 for the boy under threats to burn out his eyes and murder him, induced Mr. Willgardt to offer the reward.

Mr. McCormick has accepted the offer with tears of gratitude. He says he could not even raise $200 ransom.

## Saint Louis Post Dispatch cont

Chief of Detectives Titus, though his men have been on the case for four days without finding the boy or a definite clew to his whereabouts, is firm in his conviction that the boy has run away. Capt. James Gannon of the Highbridge Station, on the other hand, believes that the boy was kidnaped.

Capt. Titus bases his theory on the report of Detective T. J. O'Connell, who conversed with a conductor of Bay Ridge car running from Thirty-ninth street ferry, Brooklyn, to Coney Island. The conductor said that on Thursday morning a lad answering Willie McCormick's description rode on his car to Sheepshead Bay.

He was an unusually bright lad and told the conductor he had run away from his home, at 133d street and Eighth avenue, where his father kept a florist store, to go to the Buffalo Bill show at Ambrose Park. He had spent Wednesday at the Wild West camp and was going down "to see the horses."

The conductor identified the boy from the newspaper pictures of Willie McCormick.

To support the theory that the boy would run away from home, Capt. Titus quotes the statement of Father Mullen of the Sacred Heart Church, which the lad attended, that Willie was a bad boy. The captain adds that his men learned from Willie's companions that he was frequently on the streets until 10 o'clock at night, and could whip any boy of his size in High Bridge.

"I am following a clew out of town that may lead to developments," said the detective chief today. "But you can quote me as saying that the boy ran away from home. I consider the letters sent to his father a cruel hoax."

In opposition to the runaway theory, the McCormick family point out the discrepancies in the story of the Brooklyn street car man.

He had no money and as proof positive that he had no intention of running away they say that when he returned for his overcoat, he went to the dining room table where his mother's purse, containing $6 and some small change, lay open. Had he any intention of leaving home to go to a

### *Saint Louis Post Dispatch cont'*

> wild west show, he would certainly have helped himself to the money.
>
> Besides, they assert in contradiction of the statements that the boy is wild, he was so timid he would not sleep in his room at night unless the door to his mother's room adjoining was left open.
>
> They point out that the picture of the boy printed early in the week was taken two years ago and did not bear a striking resemblance to him. Willie's playmates don't support the statements that he was "scrappy" and they emphasize the fact that he was afraid to be out after dark alone.
>
> Since the receipt of the letters threatening to "burn out the boy's eyes" unless $200 was paid, McCormick and his wife have been prostrated. The shock coming after days and nights of anxiety unnerved them completely and they have had to have a doctor's care.

**The various images of Willie printed in newspapers across America differed so much, that the public became confused as to what Little Willie actually looked** like.

WILLIE M'CORMICK.

## The Boston Globe April 6, 1901

### RECEIVES ANOTHER LETTER.

#### Father of Willie McCormick Must Pay $200 Under Severe Penalty.

NEW YORK, April 5—A letter purporting to come from the kidnappers of Willie McCormick, warning his father that unless $200 was left at Central bridge and 161st st at 11 tonight the boy's ears would be found on the McCormick doorstep, was one of the important developments in the strange case today.

The letter was in the same handwriting as that of the preceding communication. Mr McCormick immediately notified the police. They put little faith in its genuineness, and told the father he need pay no attention to it.

Nevertheless Mr McCormick went to the place designated at 10 tonight, but waited in vain for any news of his missing son.

## The Birmingham News April 6, 1901

### MYSTERY OF A MISSING BOY.

#### Willie McCormick Not Yet Returned to His Home.

New York, April 5.—Notwithstanding the statements made by Captain Titus, of the Detective Bureau, that detectives would return Willie McCormick to his parents within a short time, the boy who disappeared from his home in High Bridge nine days ago, had not returned up to 1 o'clock today, nor had any trace of his whereabouts been discovered. The mystery surrounding the disappearance of the boy deepens with time and all efforts to unravel are hindered by the many conflicting stories told.

*The Omaha Daily News April 6, 1901 (Nebraska)*

# PLOT TO CAPTURE KIDNAPPERS FAILS

## Threatening Demand for Ransom for Willie McCormick Is Turned Over to Police.

## WOULD BURN CHILD'S EYES

New York, April 6.—A demand for $200 in gold accompanied by the threat that Willie McCormick's eyes would be burned out has plunged the McCormick family of High Bridge, into greater fear and anxiety than at any time since the mysterious disappearance of the boy a week ago. Both of the parents are prostrated both at the threats and at the failure of a plan to capture the kidnappers.

The letter read:

"Dear Mr. McCormick—I have kidnapped your William. Now I want you to get $200 in gold and put the money in a red cloth and then tie it up and put

## -con't The Omaha Daily News April 6, 1901

the little packet in a square pail at the northeast corner of Third avenue and East One Hundred and Thirty-fifth street. Don't tell the police. If you do we will burn the boy's eyes out, and if you put the money there and don't tell the police you will have your boy in thirty-eight hours. And if you refuse our offer we will burn the boy's eyes out and burn him to death. Yours truly,

"KIDNAPPED."

### Postal Card Follows.

In the same mail was a postal card written in the same handwriting and giving further instructions as to how the money should be left at the place mentioned. It read:

"Dear Sir—I forgot in the letter how to come at Third avenue and East One Hundred and Thirty-fifth street. The square pail is in the large boiler on northeast corner, and do not come before 8 p. m. tonight. Yours truly,

"KID."

The handwriting was of an illiterate person, and indicated that the writer was either very young or very old, for there was a marked wavering in the scrawl.

The directions in the letter were carried out by the police, but the miscreants failed to fall into the trap.

The father of Oscar Wilgerodt, a playmate of the McCormick boy, has offered $1,000 reward for the safe return of the youngster.

## New York Times April 8, 1901

# WILLIE McCORMICK NOT HOME.

### His Mother Goes to Church and Prays for His Return.

Easter came and went, and Mrs. McCormick's boy did not come home to her in High Bridge. Last night saw the mother almost a nervous wreck. Despite the orders of her physician and against the remonstrance of her husband and daughters, the agonized mother insisted on going to Easter mass.

"God will hear me," she said. "God will be good and send Willie home to me. I know he'll come home for Easter."

But he did not come. A hundred times the mother went to the door and looked out. When she was no longer able to do so she insisted on one of the girls looking out. It was a most pathetic watch, and neighbors and friends who called during the day to offer sympathy and speak a word of encouragement and hope were moved to tears.

Capt. Titus and his detectives have resumed work on the case. He has put additional men at work to follow up the kidnapping theory.

It is believed Mrs. McCormick may lose her mind if some trace of the boy, either dead or alive, be not found to relieve her suspense. She has the sympathy of everybody for miles around, and every development in the case is watched with absorbing interest by these people.

## *The Buffalo Enquirer April 8, 1901*

### MISSING BOY MAY BE AT CONEY.

#### Police of Precinct by Sea Spend a Busy Sunday Looking for Willie McCormick.

Willie McCormick, the missing Highbridge boy, maybe at Coney Island. The local police spent all of yesterday looking for the missing lad. They traced him from place to place, but could not catch him. Detectives Hauman and Lynch are at work on the case. Last Saturday afternoon Acting Captain Woods, of the Coney Island Station, received information to the effect that the McCormick boy had been seen in the vicinity of the Gravesend race-track. From a trainer they learned that a boy had applied to a number of stables at the track for employment. They found a boy named Willie McCormick and they were about to take him away with them when his father a trainer at the track appeared and he was allowed to go. He looks but little like the missing boy.

Over in Sheephead Bay, Capt. Lawson has learned within the last day that a boy now believed to be Willie McCormick sought employment from a trainer named Needham at the Sheepshead Bay track. Needham, who had read the stories of the missing boy, tried to hold him until a policeman could be sent for. Before one could arrive, however, the boy had disappeared. The police of Coney Island are firmly convinced that the McCormick boy is somewhere about the Island, and are bending every effort to get him.

# Kidnappings Skyrocket

During the waning years of the 19th Century and the early years of the 20th Century kidnappings across America skyrocketed. The hardest-hit areas were cities with large populations of hardworking European immigrants.

Kidnapping children in Europe was so common, it rarely made local newspapers. Extortionists would simply grab the child of a local merchant and demand, what they would call, a reasonable fee for the return of the child.

Every ethnic group from every part of the world, no matter how good their society, or country was; had criminals living and feeding off the honest men and women looking for a better life for themselves and their children.

And who better to extort money from?

These criminals targeted the people they knew best. They victimized the men and women from their homeland.

Italian criminals preyed mostly upon their Italian-speaking countrymen. In the 1900s hearing the word "Black Hand" or getting a letter with a "Black Hand" drawn on it, instantly instilled fear from those unfortunate men and women who received such a message. The brutal history and reputations of the various crime syndicates in the countries they had left had stayed with them when they came to America.

The Irish gangs usually did not resort to kidnapping. Their means of stealing money from their own people varied.

Irish immigrants, commonly referred to as "Greenhorns," were often fleeced by smiling red-headed con-artists with Irish brogues who were waiting patiently for them as they departed the ferries from Ellis Island.

These well-dressed thugs would meet and greet the arriving "Greenhorns" with promises of employment. However, woe to the poor fellow who fell for the enticing offer. Within a few blocks of the waterfront docks, they'd be beaten and robbed of all their worldly possessions, which often included their shoes and all the clothes on their backs.

Thugs, con men, thieves, and swindlers often met new immigrants when they arrived in Manhattan on ferries from Ellis Island.

Those trusting immigrants, who believed they had just met a kind stranger, usually woke up a few hours later in a dark alleyway with no money, no belongings, and a big lump on their heads.

New York Times April 8, 1901

# WILLIE McCORMICK NOT HOME.

## His Mother Goes to Church and Prays for His Return.

Easter came and went, and Mrs. McCormick's boy did not come home to her in High Bridge. Last night saw the mother almost a nervous wreck. Despite the orders of her physician and against the remonstrance of her husband and daughters, the agonized mother insisted on going to Easter mass.

"God will hear me," she said. "God will be good and send Willie home to me. I know he'll come home for Easter."

But he did not come. A hundred times the mother went to the door and looked out. When she was no longer able to do so she insisted on one of the girls looking out. It was a most pathetic watch, and neighbors and friends who called during the day to offer sympathy and speak a word of encouragement and hope were moved to tears.

Capt. Titus and his detectives have resumed work on the case. He has put additional men at work to follow up the kidnapping theory.

It is believed Mrs. McCormick may lose her mind if some trace of the boy, either dead or alive, be not found to relieve her suspense. She has the sympathy of everybody for miles around, and every development in the case is watched with absorbing interest by these people.

## Little Willie's Mother

Mrs. Margaret McCormick was Born in Ireland in 1853 and emigrated to the USA in 1863. Margaret was the mother of twelve children, eleven girls, and one boy.

The 1900 Federal census stated that Margaret and William had been married 26 years in 1900.

Name:     Margaret Mc Cormick
Age:  50
Birth Date: Jan 1841
Birthplace: Ireland
Home in 1900:    Bronx, New York, New York
Street:     Ogden Avenue
House Number:  1046
Race: White
Gender: Female
Immigration Year:         1863
Relation to Head of House:      Spouse
Marital Status:            Married
Spouse's Name:             William Mc Cormick
Marriage Year:    1874
Years Married:        26
Father's Birthplace:     Ireland
Mother's Birthplace:     Ireland
Years in US:        37
Naturalization:    Naturalized
Can Read:  Yes
Can Write: Yes
Can Speak English:     Yes
House Owned or Rented:     Own

Home Free or Mortgaged:    Mortgaged

| Household Members | Age | Relationship |
|---|---|---|
| William Mc Cormick | 59 | Head |
| Margaret Mc Cormick | 48 | Wife |
| Rose Mc Cormick | 31 | Daughter |
| Marcella Mc Cormick | 24 | Daughter |
| Margaret Mc Cormick | 22 | Daughter |
| Anna Mc Cormick | 20 | Daughter |
| Susan Mc Cormick | 18 | Daughter |
| Carmelita Mc Cormick | 15 | Daughter |
| Sarah Mc Cormick | 13 | Daughter |
| Gertrude Mc Cormick | 12 | Daughter |
| William Mc Cormick | 9 | Son |
| Beatrice Mc Cormick | 7 | Daughter |
| Isabell Mc Cormick | 5 | Daughter |

## *The Washington Times April 9, 1901*

**Uncle of the Missing Boy in This City Leaves Tonight for New York—Thinks His Nephew Was Kidnapped—Letters Demanding Ransom.**

The search for Willie McCormick, ten years old, reported missing for twelve days from his home at High Bridge, N. Y., has extended to this city. M. G. McCormick, a broker at the corner of Ninth and G Streets northwest, and an uncle of the boy, is preparing to go to New York to assist in the search, while Inspector Boardman, of the local police, is in communication with Captain Titus, of New York, with a view to finding trace of the lost boy.

The parents and friends of the boy scout the idea that he may have run away from home to follow the races or other aggregation, as advanced by the New York police more than a week ago. They adhere to the theory that the boy has been kidnapped, and bring forward many circumstances in support of this contention.

Several days after the boy disappeared word was received at the local Police Headquarters from the New York police asking that diligent search be made for him. His description was given and was included in the daily bulletin of the local department. A detective was sent to the Benning race track to see whether the boy had arrived there with the horses, and other routine steps were taken to locate him. Shortly afterward Mr. McCormick, of this city, called on Inspector Boardman to ask that the search be prosecuted. Mr. McCormick went over the matter thoroughly, and was told that every effort would be made to find the child. Friday last Mr. McCormick again called at Headquarters, but was told that nothing had yet developed as a clue on which the local police could work.

## cont—*Washington Times April 9, 1901*

On the night of March 27, about 7:30 o'clock, Willie McCormick started to church with two sisters. After leaving home, and when near the High Bridge Catholic Church, the boy felt the need of his overcoat, and decided to return home for it. Leaving his sisters in sight of the church, he turned homeward, and nobody has seen him since. All trace of the boy was lost in the two blocks between the church and his home.

A number of letters, bearing no signatures and written in various ways, have been received by the father of the missing boy, offering to return him. In every instance a reward of $200 in gold is demanded in the letters. The first letter received, demanded that the money be placed in a tin box, and left in an old boiler, at East 135th Street and Third Avenue, New York. Mr. McCormick placed the money as directed, and then retired, while several detectives watched the spot from a place of concealment. Nobody came to claim the reward.

Another letter was more threatening. It was to the effect that the ears of the boy would be cut off, and mailed to the distracted parents, unless $200 in gold was left on Central Bridge, New York, at 10 o'clock at night, April 4. Again the money was placed and watch kept, but no one came for the money.

## *The Democratic Chronicle April 9, 1901*

**Willie McCormick Still Missing.**

New York, April 8.—The whereabouts of the missing Willie McCormick are still unknown. The police of Red Bank, N. J., to-day thought they had discovered the lad in the person of a boy seen with a man who was begging in that town. It turned out, however, that the Red Bank strangers were William Healy and his son, of Trenton, who were on their way to Long Branch. A New York city detective and a playmate of the McCormick boy visited Red Bank this afternoon, and the playmate at once said the stranger was not the missing McCormick boy.

*Sacred Heart Church circa 1900*

*Wilkes Barre Times-Leader April 10, 1901*

# WILLIE M'CORMICK SAID TO BE SAFE

## Missing Boy Said to Have been Seen by Newsboys.

### Their Story is That He Ran Away From Home With Five Dollars and Has Since Pawned His Jewelry—He Promises to Return.

New York, April 10.—Willie McCormick, the 10-year-old son of William McCormick, Sr., who disappeared mysteriously from his home in High Bridge on the evening of March 27, is in the city.

The little fellow, whose strange disappearance has caused so much excitement, has been in New York ever since he left home, according to newsboys around Broadway and Thirty-fourth street, with whom he has been associating.

Two days ago Willie made the acquaintance of "Farmer" Bennett, one of the best known newsboys in the city. He made no secret of his identity and told Bennett about his experiences while wandering about the streets of the city.

The night on which he left home, ostensibly to overtake his sisters on the way to church, the boy said he picked up a $5 bill which lay on a mantel, and with this money he bought food and kept from actual want until yesterday.

## *Wilkes Barre Times-Leader cont'*

### Pawned His Overcoat.

After this money had been spent Willie disposed of his light overcoat in a pawnshop. He had been trying for several days to get some employment with the Wild West show at Madison Square Garden. He discussed his aspirations with "Farmer" Bennett and other newsboys and displayed keen interest in the notoriety which his disappearance had given to him.

Captain Chapman, accompanied by his ward man, Wesley Hall, and Johnny Quinn, one of Willie McCormick's former companions, went to Madison Square Garden last night looking for the missing boy.

Edward Coath, another newsboy, had written a letter saying that he had met Willie McCormick and that Willie had shown him a book and pencil which he had said his sister had given to him. Captain Chapman got no trace of the McCormick boy, but he found Coath, with whom he talked for some time. The captain returned to the High Bridge station late last evening, believing that the boy Coath had talked with was not Mr. McCormick's missing son.

## *Wilkes Barre Times-Leader cont'*

**Promised to Go Home.**

"Farmer" Bennett, who had talked with Willie several times during the last few days, met him again yesterday near Broadway and Thirty-fourth street. The newsboy reminded Willie of the keen anxiety of his father as to his safety and told him that his mother had been made seriously ill because of his continued absence from home.

Bennett pleaded with Willie to return to his home at once and end the suspense of his parents and sisters.

After listening to the words of his new found friend Willie half promised to return to his home last night. He wanted Bennett to go with him, and this wish the newsboy consented to gratify. It was arranged that they should meet at 7 o'clock last night and go at once to the McCormick home. But when the hour came Bennett could not find Willie at the place agreed upon.

## The Buffalo Evening News April 10, 1901

# MISSING BOY WAS SEEN BY A HACKMAN.

### Believes He Took the McCormick Youth and Two Others to the Station.

(By Associated Press.)

PROVIDENCE, R. I., April 10.—Edward Costigan, a hack driver in this city, believes he had the missing Willie McCormick and two other persons as passengers in this city about a week ago. He states that he is not certain just what day it was, but he has grown very confident in the belief that the boy was the missing son of Florist McCormick.

The trio comprised a boy about 16 years old, a young woman about 22 and an elderly man. They called upon him at the Union Station in the center of the city to take them to the station of the Providence, Fall River & Bristol railroad at Fox Point. When the destination was reached and the cabman opened the hack door, he says the boy was looking at a picture of the missing McCormick boy in a newspaper and Costigan says the boy remarked: "They think I am lost, but I ain't; I'm going home." He says the boy acted dull and "dopey."

## Passaic Daily News April 10, 1901

# WILLIE M'CORMICK SAFE

### Newsboys Say They Saw Him as Recently as Yesterday.

## SAID HE TOOK AWAY FIVE DOLLARS

**On That and by Pawning His Overcoat He Has Managed to Get Along Thus Far—Has Promised to Return to His Home.**

New York, April 10.—Willie McCormick, the 10-year-old son of William McCormick, Sr., who disappeared mysteriously from his home in High Bridge on the evening of March 27, is in the city.

The little fellow, whose strange disappearance has caused so much excitement, has been in New York ever since he left home, according to newsboys around Broadway and Thirty-fourth street, with whom he has been associating.

Two days ago Willie made the acquaintance of "Farmer" Bennett, one of the best known newsboys in the city. He made no secret of his identity and told Bennett about his experiences while wandering about the streets of the city.

The night on which he left home, ostensibly to overtake his sisters on the way to church, the boy said he picked up a $5 bill which lay on a mantel, and with this money he bought food and kept from actual want until yesterday.

*-cont—Passaic Daily News*

**Pawned His Overcoat.**

After this money had been spent Willie disposed of his light overcoat in a pawnshop. He had been trying for several days to get some employment with the Wild West show at Madison Square Garden. He discussed his aspirations with "Farmer" Bennett and other newsboys and displayed keen interest in the notoriety which his disappearance had given to him.

Captain Chapman, accompanied by his ward man, Wesley Hall, and Johnny Quinn, one of Willie McCormick's former companions, went to Madison Square Garden last night looking for the missing boy.

Edward Coath, another newsboy, had written a letter saying that he had met Willie McCormick and that Willie had shown him a book and pencil which he had said his sister had given to him. Captain Chapman got no trace of the McCormick boy, but he found Coath, with whom he talked for some time. The captain returned to the High Bridge station late last evening, believing that the boy Coath had talked with was not Mr. McCormick's missing son.

## -cont—Passaic Daily News

### Promised to Go Home.

"Farmer" Bennett, who had talked with Willie several times during the last few days, met him again yesterday near Broadway and Thirty-fourth street. The newsboy reminded Willie of the keen anxiety of his father as to his safety and told him that his mother had been made seriously ill because of his continued absence from home.

Bennett pleaded with Willie to return to his home at once and end the suspense of his parents and sisters.

After listening to the words of his new found friend Willie half promised to return to his home last night. He wanted Bennett to go with him, and this wish the newsboy consented to gratify. It was arranged that they should meet at 7 o'clock last night and go at once to the McCormick home. But when the hour came Bennett could not find Willie at the place agreed upon.

## The Yonkers Statesman April 10, 1901

### That Kidnapped Boy.

PROVIDENCE, R. I., April 10.—Edward Costigan, a hackdriver in this city, believes he had the missing Willie McCormick and two other persons as passengers about a week ago.

## *The Buffalo Enquirer April 11, 1901*

### KIDNAPING MYSTERIES BECOMING DEEPER.

#### Efforts to Find Willie McCormick and Lena Sack Unavailing.

New York, April 11.—The police admitted yesterday that the case of Willie McCormick, who disappeared from his home two weeks ago, is wrapped in deeper mystery than ever. Every clue that looked promising has been run out without avail.

The same is true in the case of Lena Sack, the 5-year-old girl, who disappeared from her home on the East Side Saturday. The latest theory in the case is that the girl was murdered.

## *The Lola Register April 11, 1901 (Kansas)*

### STILL NO NEWS FROM HIM

#### Disappearance of Willie McCormack is Still a Mystery.

By Scripps-McRae Press Association.

New York, April 11.—The police admit today that the disappearance of Willie McCormack, aged eleven, is wrapped in as deep mystery as ever. The boy disappeared a fortnight ago, probably kidnapped, and the reward of ten thousand dollars has resulted in nothing.

## *The Scranton Tribune* April 12, 1901

# KIDNAPPERS WILL GET A REWARD

### A Thousand Dollars Will Be Paid for the Return of Willie McCormick, and No Questions Asked.

By Exclusive Wire from The Associated Press.

New York, April 11.—A reward of $1,000 will probably be offered within a day or two to the kidnappers of Willie McCormick, if they return the boy. This ransom will be offered by an uncle of the boy, Michael C. McCormick, of Washington, D. C., according to a story he told at police headquarters today.

The reward Mr. McCormick purposes offering, if the police think best, and he says it will be with the understanding that there will be no questions asked and that the kidnappers will not be prosecuted.

## *The Monmouth Enquire* April 12, 1901

### Not Willie McCormick.

Monday morning the Red Bank police arrested a boy and a tramp who were begging there. They thought the boy might be Willie McCormick, the High Bridge lad who was kidnapped a short time ago. The boy appeared frightened and said he was Willie Ely of Trenton. The tramp refused to talk, so the New York police were notified, and Detective Tinker and one of Willie McCormick's companions went to Red Bank, but found that the boy wasn't Willie. The man and boy were then released.

## *The Standard Union April 12, 1901*

### REWARD FOR MISSING BOY

#### Uncle of Willie McCormick Searches the Tenderloin.

Michael G. McCormick, an uncle of the missing boy, William McCormick, and a broker of Washington, D. C., if what he said at Police Headquarters, Manhattan, yesterday is true, will within a few days offer a reward of $1,000 for the recovery of his lost nephew.

Accompanied by two detectives from the Highbridge police station, another from Police Headquarters and a newsboy as a guide, William McCormick spent the greater part of yesterday searching the Tenderloin for his lost boy. A detective from Police Headquarters joined them, and after a brief search in Broadway and Sixth avenue they found a newsboy who said he had seen a boy who looked like William McCormick, but the search was futile.

## *The Evening Review April 12, 1901, Liverpool Ohio*

The New York police admit that the case of Willie McCormick, who disappeared from his home two weeks ago, is wrapped in deeper mystery than ever. Every clue that looked promising has been run down without avail. The same is true in the case of Lena Pensak, the 5-year-old girl who disappeared from her home on the East Side Saturday.

## *New York Times* April 13, 1901

### BOY LIKE McCORMICK HELD.

#### Yonkers Police Thought They Had the Missing Lad—New York Man Also Held.

YONKERS, N. Y., April 12.—For a time to-day the police thought they might have Willie McCormick. The boy turned out not to be the missing High Bridge lad, but a boy and man are held while an investigation is to be made.

Patrolman Buckhout saw a man and a boy alight from a car from Mount Vernon. The boy was crying and seemed to be frightened. In a general way he answered the description of Willie McCormick. Buckhout asked the man where they were going and the man replied, "To a hotel." On being questioned, the boy said he did not know the man. Buckhout took both to the police station.

The boy said he was Michael Demonte, thirteen years of age, of 131 Mulberry Street, New York. The man described himself as Earl C. Young of 103 West Fifty-eighth Street, New York. Their stories agreed in that the man had picked up the boy in front of the Pulitzer Building on Park Row about 1 o'clock this morning while the boy was selling papers. For a consideration the boy accompanied the man. He was to distribute samples of a patent glue in this city.

The man said he intended the boy no harm, and picked him up supposing he had no home and meant to dress him well and employ him as a distributor. Both have been committed until Monday or later.

## *The Morning News April 13, 1901*

> Detective Petrosini, the Italian sleuth of the Central Office, was detailed on the case yesterday for the purpose of running down this story. He reported to Captain Titus last night that he could get no verification of the story. The Italian who was said to have figured in the case had left High Bridge, and the detective was told to make an effort to find him.

Detective Petrosino was a pioneer in the fight against organized crime in the United States. He was murdered in 1909 while secretly investigating the Sicilian Mafia in Palermo.

### *The Marion Star April 16, 1901*

**WAS HE WILLIE M'CORMICK?**

Binghamton, N. Y., April 15.—A farmer living near New Milford, Pa., reports that a boy answering perfectly the description of Willie McCormick, the missing New York boy, worked for him last week.

Saturday night he paid the lad and he disappeared.

### *The Boston Globe April 15, 1901*

The relatives and friends of the missing boy, Willie McCormick, have offered rewards aggregating $2000 for his return, with no response. It is safe to bet that the boy has run away.

### *The Meridian Daily Journal April 15, 1901*

## BIG REWARD.

New York, April 16.—Rewards aggregating ..6,000 are now offered for the safe return of Willie McCormick, missing from his High Bridge home for nearly three weeks. The lad's uncle, Michael G. McCormick, a wealthy Washington man, offers $5,000. Oscar Wilgerodt, a neighbor, offers the other $1,000. Wilgerodt has taken a deep interest in the case because his own son, a lad of ten, and the missing boy were playmates and the son tearfully pleaded with him to find Willie.

*Minneapolis Journal April 16, 1901*

## WILLIE NEAR BOSTON

**Letter Purports to Be From the McCormick Kidnappers.**

*New York Sun Special Service.*

New York, April 16.—Michael G. McCormick, uncle of the missing Highbridge boy, offers $5,000 reward for his return and Oscar Wilgerodt, cloak manufacturer, a neighbor of McCormick's, offers $1,000. Both are convinced that the lad was kidnapped.

The latest clue received by the family was a letter from Boston. The writer related that he and two other men captured Willie at Birch street and Ogden avenue, in Highbridge, the night he left home. The letter says that the boy was taken to a point near Boston.

When Little Willie McCormick disappeared in March of 1901, the first and most prevalent assumption on the minds of all was; that the boy was kidnapped. At that time in American history, kidnapping a child for ransom had reached epidemic proportions.

The crime of kidnapping exploded with the wave of immigrants coming from Europe to the USA during the late 19th and early 20th centuries. It was considered by small-time criminals as a fail-safe way to make a few bucks. If the ransom was not exorbitant, most criminals knew a child's family would pay and not bother to get the police involved, for fear of a mishap.

And let us remember, in 1900 the police did not have the tools or the trained personnel to handle the number of kidnappings being committed around the country. And besides, many of the kidnappings were from different criminal organizations that came along for the ride with certain ethnic groups. One such organization was known as, the "Black Hand" which was a criminal society that arrived in America with a massive influx of hardworking and family-orientated Italians.

## *The Akron News April 17, 1901*

### A MISSING BOY'S FATE.

**Believed to Have Been Stolen by an Italian Laborer For Revenge.**

New York, April 17.—The police of High Bridge station discovered last night what they believe is a promising clew to the mysterious disappearance of Willie McCormick, and as a result detectives were engaged last night in searching the Italian quarter in the Bronx for an Italian who disappeared at the same time as the boy. Colonies in the city are also being searched.

This Italian, with a number of others, was engaged in the erection of a new building directly opposite the McCormick home in Ogden avenue. Mr. McCormick has had considerable trouble with the laborers, as they entered his yard at the noon hour and sat under the shadow of his fence to eat their dinners. Mr. McCormick frequently complained about the nuisance and threatened to cause the arrest of some of the laborers unless the nuisance was abated.

One of the laborers, whose name the police have learned, finally engaged in a row with the father of the missing boy and a few days later disappeared from his work at the same time that the boy disappeared. It is said that the Italian threatened to "get even" with Mr. McCormick.

### *The Dayton Herald April 18, 1901*

# PAT SHEEDY TO ACT AS GO-BETWEEN

### OFFERS $5,000 FOR RESTORATION OF WILLIE McCORMICK, AND PROMISES THAT KIDNAPERS SHALL NOT BE PROSECUTED.

New York, April 18.—Pat Sheedy, known the world over as the gambler who has never broken his word, has taken a hand in the McCormick kidnaping case. He will act as a go-between, between the kidnapers and Michael McCormick, uncle of the missing boy, and friend of the gambler. Sheedy is the man who recently recovered the stolen Gainsborough picture.

The following statement was made today as a result of the conference between McCormick and Sheedy.

"Notice—To Whom It May Concern: This is to say that I am empowered to pay $5,000 for information that will result in restoring Willie McCormick to his parents. I give my word of honor that all dealings to this end will be treated as strictly confidential and in good faith.

"The money will be paid by me personally when I am enabled to deliver the boy. I have accepted this commission on the condition that no person shall be harmed.  P. F. SHEEDY."

### *Wilkes Barre Times-Leader April 18, 1901*

### BELIEVE THE BOY IS DEAD.

### Parents of "Willie" McCormick Think He Was Murdered and Buried in Sewer.

The parents of Willie McCormick, the boy who has been strangely missing for a month, and who is believed to have been kidnapped, are of the opinion to-day that their son was murdered, and his body now lies buried in the excavation of an up-town sewer in Manhattan. The basis for this theory is the fact that "Willie," with another boy, plagued an Italian on the day of the boy's disappearance, and the Italian vowed vengeance. The police are looking for this man and the boy's father will have the recently closed excavation reopened and a search made for the body.

## The Brooklyn Times Union April 19, 1901

**Catholic Priest Offers $10,000 Reward for Recovery of Willie McCormick.**

## The Chicago Tribune April 20, 1901

**$10,000 REWARD FOR A KIDNAPER!**

**Father Mullin Offers a Fortune for Capture of the Abductor of Willie McCormick and Return of the Boy.**

(By Associated Press)

NEW YORK, April 20.—"I will give $10,000 for the capture of the kidnaper of little Willie McCormick and the return of the led to his parents."

This announcement is made by Father James A. Mullin of the Church of the Sacred Heart, Highbridge, to which the lad of 10 years was on his way three weeks ago when he disappeared. The priest had a long talk with the boy's mother, and her grief impressed him so keenly that he declared that nothing should stand in the way of finding the boy.

All the boy's family, his mother, his father and his sisters, are on the verge of despair. The neighbors say that at all hours of the night Mrs. McCormick wanders about the grounds around her home calling the boy's name.

Father James Mullin

Why would the pastor of the small Bronx Church offer to give a $10,000 reward for the return of little Willie McCormick? And where would the money come from? Did Father Mullin even have access to that amount of money?

Was it a genuine offer? Or did the Priest know something that no one else knew?

In 1901, $10,000 was the equivalent value of offering a reward of over $350,000 in today's dollars.

Even before Little Willie disappeared, Father Mullin showed an interest in the McCormick family. Maybe Father Mullin's interest was pure. After all, Willie's father had been absent from the home for the previous 2 years. Mr. McCormick had been serving time in a New York City Prison for swindling several investors who were backing his lucrative Manhattan Wholesale Flower Business.

Little Willie disappeared within weeks of his father returning home from prison. And while the police and half the nation were searching for Willie, Father Mullins, the Pastor of Sacred Heart Church, was reported to be spreading rumors that Mr. McCormick had, since returning home from prison, been physically abusing and beating his son for the child's misbehaviors.

The local gossip of Father Mullins spreading the story about the paternal abuse of little Willie was denied by the "Reverend Father Mullins".

*Father Jamea A. Mullin*

## Buffalo Evening News April 20, 1901

### SHEEDY IS HERE.

#### The New York Gambler is Ready to Pay the Ransom When the Boy is Returned.

When Pat Sheedy, the gambler, was shown the Associated Press dispatch this afternoon which stated that Rev. James A. Mullin of the Church of the Sacred Heart at Highbridge, New York, had offered $10,000 for the recovery of the supposedly kidnaped boy, Willie McCormick, he said:

"I do not see the use of creating a rising market in the kidnaping business. Suppose some other pastor should offer $15,000 for the recovery of the boy, or some boy like him. Wouldn't that fade the little $5000 I am empowered to pay when the boy is delivered to me?

"I know positively that I am the only person empowered to deal with this matter by the boy's parents, and all I can say is that further offers of more money will only delay matters if the boy is alive and if he was kidnaped for a ransom. I have his picture; I know questions to ask that will place his identity beyond the shadow of a doubt, but whoever has him has got to trust me, and anyone who is on the level will do so, man to man. I am not going around looking for people to claim that reward. They must come to me, either here in the Iroquois or name some place where I can meet them face to face and conduct operations personally. Perhaps the New York clergyman has been so profoundly impressed by the grief of the mother that he is willing to go to any length to get the boy back, but there isn't much use in people of his class dealing with a class about which they know nothing. I tell you frankly that I'd be the most surprised man in Buffalo or the United States if Willie McCormick is found alive. I think it would be really safe to boost the reward to $100,000. All they will get, however, for the real Willie they will get from Pat Sheedy, in my estimation.

"I have come to Buffalo to stay if the authorities will let me, and I shall put up here at the Iroquois for the present. I guess the landlord won't kick as long as I put up the markers. I have not opened communication with anyone about the boy and don't expect to. I am not looking for letters about the case. The money that I offer for his return is in my clothes ready to be paid when the boy is found and restored. No questions will be asked. No, I do not expect to be arrested. There is not the slightest ground for such a course on the part of the police. I doubt whether the boy is living. He did not run away, in my opinion. I shall treat his captors squarely, if he was taken by any one, just as I acted squarely about the Gainsborough picture. I have always done just as I agreed and I challenge anyone to show the contrary in a single instance."

Sheedy has the appearance in figure, countenance and bearing of a highly cultivated church dignitary and expressed his pleasure at meeting a representative of the NEWS, cordially inviting him to call at any time when seeking information on matters within Sheedy's knowledge.

*New York Times April 20, 1901*

## MAY BE YOUNG McCORMICK.

### Boy Answering Description Seen with Five Men Near Philadelphia.

*Special to The New York Times.*

PHILADELPHIA, Penn., April 19.—Willie McCormick, the missing New York boy, is believed to be in hiding with his abductors on the outskirts of this city.

A boy answering the description of the stolen child begged for food yesterday morning at the home of Henry B. Duncan, near Bellevue, a town adjacent to Wilmington. Having received food the boy rejoined five men who hovered in a small woods near by. Mr. Duncan notified Chief of Police Massey of Wilmington, who sent word to Chester and this city.

The boy and men were last seen tramping north, and it is thought that they may have reached the vicinity of Darby and Cobb's Creek by this time, a locality which affords not a few hiding places.

*The Philadelphia Enquirer April 20, 1901*

# POSITIVE IT WAS M'CORMICK BOY

## A New York Oculist Declares Lad Who Asked for Position Was the One Wanted

NEW YORK, April 19.—According to Dr. Henri P. Alexander, an oculist of this city, the missing Willie McCormick is in this city.

Dr. Alexander said to-day that last Tuesday afternoon he was in the office of Dr. Archibald Veinberg, when a boy called and asked for a position.

"I asked him his name," said the physician, "and he said it was Willie Mac and hesitated. I asked him again and he answered it was Willie McKerr. I asked him where he worked and he replied 'In a cake factory.' I thought nothing more of the matter until yesterday when I saw the missing McCormick boy's picture in an evening paper. I concluded I had seen the face somewhere, but could not remember the place. At 8 o'clock last night Dr. Veinberg called me on the telephone and asked me if I remembered about the boy who had called at the office last Tuesday. I replied that I did. 'I am sure that boy was Willie McCormick,' said Dr. Veinberg.

"Both of us are positive that the boy was the missing Willie McCormick."

## *The Minneapolis Journal April 20, 1901*

# PASTOR OFFERS REWARD

## CLUE TO WILLIE McCORMICK

### Boy Was Begging for Food, and He Is Thought to Be Near Philadelphia.

**New York Sun Special Service**

New York, April 20.—Rev. J. A. Mullen, pastor of the Roman Catholic church of the Sacred Heart in Highbridge, where the McCormick family attend, has offered an additional reward of $10,000 for the return of the missing Willie McCormick, and the arrest of his kidnappers. Father Mullen's offer brings the total reward up to $16,000, of which $5,000 is offered by an uncle of Willie McCormick, and $1,000 by the boy's father, who is in comparatively poor circumstances.

A dispatch from Philadelphia says a boy answering the description of Willie McCormick begged for food Thursday at the home of Henry B. Duncan, near Wilmington. Having received food, he rejoined five men. They were last seen tramping northward. It is believed they may have reached the vicinity of Darby, a suburb of Philadelphia, and the police are looking for them.

## *The Reading Times April 20, 1901*

# NEW YORK POLICE FAIL AS USUAL.

THEY CAN SECURE NO TRACE OF THE TEN-YEAR-OLD BOY WHO DISAPPEARED THREE WEEKS AGO AND NOW PHILADELPHIA TAKES A TURN.

Philadelphia, April 19.—Willie McCormick, the ten-year-old New York boy, who was recently kidnaped for a ransom, and whose disappearance was heralded in the newspapers, is believed to be in hiding with his abductors on the outskirts of this city.

A boy answering the description of the stolen child begged for food yesterday morning at the home of Henry B. Duncan, near Bellevue, a town adjacent to Wilmington. Having received food, the boy rejoined five men who hovered in a small woods near by. Mr. Duncan notified Chief of Police Massey, of Wilmington, who sent word to Chester and this city. The boy and men were last seen tramping north, and it is thought they may have reached the vicinity of Darby and Cobb's creek by this time, a locality which affords not a few hiding places. The police of this city, Wilmington and Chester are keeping a sharp lookout for the party.

—o—

## *The Reading Times cont'*

### FEAR LAD WAS MURDERED.

#### His Parents Think an Italian May Have Killed Him.

New York, April 19.—The parents of Willie McCormick, the boy who has been strangely missing for a month, and who is believed to have been kidnaped, are of the opinion today that their son was murdered and that his body now lies buried in the excavation for an uptown sewer. The basis for this theory is the fact that Willie, with another boy, plagued an Italian on the day of the boy's disappearance, and the Italian vowed vengeance.

The police are now looking for this man, and the boy's father will have the recent excavation reopened and a search made.

### BOY'S UNCLE IN WASHINGTON.

Washington, April 19.—Michael G. McCormick, the uncle of Willie McCormick, the missing boy of High Bridge, N. Y., is in Washington running down all clues that may lead to the writer of the "A. E. C." letter dated Washington, which he received yesterday. "A. E. C." makes inquiries about the reward promised for the return of the boy. Mr. McCormick was in conference here today with the chief of police and the post office inspectors, and they will assist in the search.

## — NY Times continued

Dr. Veinberg, Dr. Alexander says, said then that the boy had just made another visit to his place, and was more confused than ever by the questions. This time he said he was self-supporting and alone. Dr. Veinberg said that when the lad left he sent an employe to follow him, but the lad saw he was watched and suddenly dashed between passing vehicles in the avenue and disappeared.

A poorly dressed but respectable appearing old man who refused his name, called at the McCormick home late yesterday and told Mr. McCormick that his boy was living under the name of Ketcham, with a Mrs. Rhylberg, at 6 Berkeley Place, Brooklyn. He seemed sure of it, and identified a photograph, and the sorrowing father made a journey to Brooklyn Police Headquarters, where he told Capt. Reynolds, in charge of the Detective Bureau, about it, and the latter detailed Detective Sergeant Brady to accompany him to the Berkeley Place house. They found a boy there working for a dressmaker, who gave the name of Ketcham, and was reticent about his antecedents, but he was not the missing lad, and Mr. McCormick returned sadly to his home, reaching there shortly before midnight.

Detectives Petrosini and Doran of Police Headquarters were in High Bridge yesterday working on the case, and the former spent his time among the Italian laborers, one of whom is believed by Mrs. McCormick to be responsible for the disappearance because her boy with others had been in the habit of teasing the men. Petrosini reported, however, that he could find none who had cherished any special animosity to the boy, and, in fact, those who remembered him agreed that he had been less aggressive than any of the others.

Patrick Sheedy, who has taken up the case, was seen at the Sturtevant House last night, just as he was starting for Buffalo. He said that he had lost faith in the kidnapping theory, and was satisfied that the boy is dead, and he leans to the theory of the mother, that he was killed by some revengeful laborer. He has received a letter referring to a boy who speaks two languages. Willie McCormick, however, only spoke one.

## —NY Times continued

"Mrs. McCormick, who has been in a very critical condition as a result of her worry, was reported to be better late last night.

Another letter to which the police and Mr. McCormick attach little credence was received yesterday, signed with the name of "Lillie Ganz." There was an address in West One Hundred and Forty-first Street appended. The letter said, "I know where your son is and will tell you if you will give me the entire reward."

Detetctives went to the house and found that a woman of that name had lived there, but had recently moved to First Avenue. They had not found her at a late hour. The letter was mailed at the same Post Office sub-station from which all the deceiving letters have come.

## MAY BE YOUNG McCORMICK.

### Boy Answering Description Seen with Five Men Near Philadelphia.

*Special to The New York Times.*

PHILADELPHIA, Penn., April 19.—Willie McCormick, the missing New York boy, is believed to be in hiding with his abductors on the outskirts of this city.

A boy answering the description of the stolen child begged for food yesterday morning at the home of Henry B. Duncan, near Bellevue, a town adjacent to Wilmington. Having received food the boy rejoined five men who hovered in a small woods near by. Mr. Duncan notified Chief of Police Massey of Wilmington, who sent word to Chester and this city.

The boy and men were last seen tramping north, and it is thought that they may have reached the vicinity of Darby and Cobb's Creek by this time, a locality which affords not a few hiding places.

## *The International Gazette April 20, 1901*

NEW YORK, April 19.—Dr. Henri P. Alexander, an oculist, and Dr. Archibald Veinberg are positive that a boy who called Tuesday at the office of Dr. Veinberg and asked for work is the missing Willie McCormick. He made unsatisfactory replies to questions and gave his name first as Willie Mac and then Willie MacKerr.

## *The Baltimore Dun April 20, 1901*

### SHEEDY AS INTERMEDIARY

**Kipnapers of McCormick Boy Can Find Him at Buffalo If They Wish to Negotiate.**

NEW YORK, April 19.—Pat Sheedy, who has agreed to act as intermediary between the kidnapers of Willie McCormick and the McCormick family in negotiations for the boy's return, made a statement yesterday in which he said:

"I am going to leave New York at 9:40 tomorrow evening for Buffalo. I am interested in the exposition and will be there all summer at the Iroquois hotel.

"My idea is that the boy was never kidnaped for a ransom. I think he was taken out of revenge. I had Mr. McCormick, the uncle of the boy, make a searching investigation relative to any trouble the boy's father or mother may have had with anyone. In this way we found out about an Italian who had a grudge against the boy. I'll give my word that the man who gives me information shall not be harmed."

## *The Courier News April 20, 1901*

### $10,000 REWARD.

**Father Mullin to Give That Sum For Willie McCormick's Captors.**

New York, April 20.—"I will give $10,000 for the capture of the kidnaper of little Willie McCormick and the return of the lad to his parents."

This announcement was made yesterday by Father James A. Mullin of the Church of the Sacred Heart, Highbridge, to which the lad of 10 years was on his way three weeks ago when he disappeared. The priest had just had a long talk with the boy's mother, and her grief had impressed him so keenly that he declared that nothing should stand in the way of finding the boy.

All the boy's family—his mother, his father and his sisters—are on the verge of despair. The neighbors say that at all hours of the night Mrs. McCormick wanders about the grounds around her home and calls, "Willie, Willie!"

*The old newspaper articles you are reading were written in 1901. The English language and the style of writing used by journalists in the nascent days of the 20th century have, to a varying degree, changed.

Terms and idioms used during those times are often misunderstood or, misinterpreted by readers today. Plus, some of the terminology and colloquialisms used by those long-deceased journalists are so archaic & obscure that it would take an etymologist to figure out the meaning.

## *New York Tribune* April 20, 1901

**AN OCULIST SAYS A LAD WHO LOOKED LIKE MISSING BOY ASKED HIM FOR A JOB.**

According to Dr. Henri P. Alexander, an oculist, of No. 24 East One-hundred-and-twenty-fifth-st., the missing William McCormick may be in this city. Dr. Alexander said yesterday afternoon that last Tuesday afternoon he was in the office of Dr. Archibald Vineberg, at Forty-second-st. and Fifth-ave., when a boy called and asked for a place. "I asked him his name," said the physician, "and he said it was Willie Mc—— and hesitated. I asked him again, and he said it was Willie McKerr. I asked him where he worked, and he replied, 'In a cake factory.' I asked him where he went to school, and he told me at St. Joseph's Home. His replies to several other questions were so unsatisfactory that I told him to go and get recommendations from his former teacher and employer, and that if they were satisfactory he could get a job.

"After the boy had left I told Dr. Vineberg that I believed the boy's replies were unsatisfactory. I thought nothing more of the matter until yesterday, when I saw the missing McCormick boy's picture in an evening paper. I concluded I had seen the face somewhere, but could not remember the place. At 8 o'clock last night Dr. Vineberg called me on the telephone and asked me if I remembered about the boy who had called at the office last Tuesday. I replied that I did. 'I am sure that boy was Willie McCormick,' said Dr. Vineberg. He then continued to tell me that the same boy had returned to his office yesterday afternoon, but as on his previous visit his answers were unsatisfactory. The boy on his first visit said he was the only support of a widowed mother, while Thursday he said he was self-supporting.

"Dr. Vineberg said that when the boy left his office yesterday he sent one of his men to watch him. Seeing that he was being followed, the boy ran up Fifth-ave. and disappeared.

"Pat" Sheedy, when seen last night at the Sturtevant House just before starting for Buffalo, said:

I was informed this evening that Mr. McCormick had a clew to his son's whereabouts and had gone to Brooklyn to investigate. This is like a dying man grasping at a straw. I don't think that William McCormick will ever be found alive, and I have lost all faith in the kidnapping theory. I lean to the theory of Willie's mother, that he has probably been done away with by some revengeful Italian.

## *New York Times* April 21, 1901

### SAYS HE SAW McCORMICK.

#### Man Declares He Met Him in Gansevoort Market Three Weeks Ago.

The Rev. James A. Mullin, pastor of the Roman Catholic Church of the Sacred Heart, in High Bridge, where the family of the missing boy, Willie McCormick, attend services, said yesterday that his offer of $10,000 reward for the return of the boy and the arrest of his kidnappers was not made on behalf of the congregation, but on his own responsibility.

Father Mullin never expects to have to pay it, as he is satisfied that the boy was not stolen, but ran away from home. He bases his belief upon a story that the boy was seen walking in Jerome Avenue two hours after his disappearance.

Broderick Smith of 58 Gansevoort Street went to Police Headquarters yesterday and told Capt. Titus of the Detective Bureau that he is sure he saw Willie McCormick and an older boy in Gansevoort Market about three weeks ago. He talked with them, but the bigger boy nudged his companion to prevent him from giving any information about themselves.

They slept in a stable near the market, he said, and had told him that they were going on to Boston the next day. He did not see them again, but readily identified a picture of Willie McCormick as that of the boy he had seen and talked to.

## *New York Times April 22, 1901*

### BY LAVINIA HART.

Pennsylvania's new bill making kidnapping a crime punishable by life imprisonment, is a worthy precedent for other states to follow.

The horrors attendant upon this crime can never be realized until one sees them at work as I saw them yesterday in the McCormick home. Three weeks have elapsed since Willie McCormick disappeared from home.

His father, a hearty, healthy man, has grown stooped beneath the weight of dread and sorrow and can scarcely speak a rational sentence; his mother, whose life has always been shielded from care by a devoted family, has aged 10 years in the 10 dreadful days; the hair over her forehead turned to white, her eyes sunken and her cheeks drawn; his sisters have wept until their pretty faces are swollen beyond recognition, and sleep comes to none in that wretched household, except from sheer exhaustion.

"If my boy were dead, laid out in this parlor, ready for the last rites, I could say 'thank God!'" said Mrs. McCormick drearily, "at least I could know he was out of misery, but this agony of terror, this fear that he is being tortured and abused!"

"Don't let her talk," said Marcvelli. McCormick; "we're afraid that she will lose her reason. I'll tell you everything we know about Willie. The police have suggested that we are keeping something back; that there might have been some trouble which would explain the boy's disappearance and justify the running away theory. Now it is just as absurd to say that Willie ran away as it would be to say he is here. I don't believe there ever could be a happier home than this one, and you can imagine that he had things pretty much his own way, being the only boy, with 11 sisters."

"What sort of books did he read?"

"He didn't read any. Sometimes on very cold nights or rainy nights the children would get around the fire in the playroom downstairs and Gertrude, who is 12 years old and devoted to Willie with her whole heart and soul, would read aloud such stories as "Little Two Eyes" an "Little Red Riding Hood.""

## Saint Louis Dispatch April 22, 1901

# REV. FATHER MULLIN WITHDRAWS HIS REWARD.

### To Escape Persecution from Fakirs and Cranks—Has Had No Peace Since He Offered $10,000 for Willie McCormick.

The $10,000 reward offered by the Rev. Father Mullin of the Church of the Sacred Heart, Highbridge, for the return of the lost Willie McCormick to his parents and the arrest of his kidnappers, was withdrawn by the priest yesterday.

Father Mullin said he had been compelled to take this action to escape a horde of mountebanks, clairvoyants, fakirs of every sort and cranks of all degrees who have besieged him since he posted the money.

"I have had no time whatever for the performance of my sacred duties since I offered the reward," said Father Mullin yesterday. "I have had letters from all over the country, and there have awaited me daily scores of persons pretending to know something of the lost lad.

"My heart bleeds for the boy's parents, and particularly for his mother. May God give her courage to bear this terrible trial. But I have withdrawn the reward temporarily, as I have work that must be attended to.

"My offer has been good for four days, and has produced no result but infinite annoyance to me. If there come any news of the boy within the next week that appears to give hope, I will at once renew my offer and increase the amount to any sum that will produce the results—the capture of the kidnappers and the return of the boy.

"However, I begin to adhere to the theory that Willie was not stolen. He either left home alone or met death in some strange way. May God return him to us soon, if he lives. If not, we pray for some news that will end this terrible suspense."

*April 22, 1901, Various Newspapers Spanning North America*

## The Family Has Received Five Notes.

Five notes, written in a cramped hand, apparently by the same illiterate person, have been received by the McCormicks. The first two came after the boy had been missing nearly five days. The writer claimed to have the boy in his possession and threatened to burn his eyes out unless $300 was left in a dark spot at Third avenue and One Hundred and Thirty-fifth street the night of April 1. The father left a dummy package at the spot indicated while detectives watched from nearby doorways. No one called for it. The next day two more of the notes were received. The substance of them was that the writer had seen the detectives, and that by the time the letter was received the boy would be with him at sea. The final letter came Thursday, saying that if a sum of money was not placed at Central Bridge and One Hundred and Sixty-first street Friday night the boy's ears would be found on the porch in the morning.

The family believed the first letters were genuine, and even the police took considerable stock in them. The receipt of the later letters, however, has created the impression that all were probably sent by some heartless crank or jester or possibly by some bitter enemy of the McCormicks.

*Cont'*

"Didn't he ever read boys' books—stories about adventures and detectives and Indian escapades?"

"Never; he was only 10 and very childish. He knew nothing of that sort of literature and, what is more, he had none of that spirit. He was the most timid of all the children. He had a horror of the dark. He would not go up to bed alone and we never dared make him sleep alone; he'd have cried himself sick. And if the boys coaxed him to remain out playing after dark—he was easily coaxed—they had to promise to bring him home to the door and he wouldn't let them leave till he got inside. Then isn't it most improbable that he would run away in the dark? Why, if you knew his temperament you would realize how impossible such a thing is."

### Taught to Be Obedient, but Not Mistreated.

"Did he like to go to school?"

"No, not particularly, but he was obedient and knew he had to go. He never played truant in his life. Besides, there was all of Easter week coming, and he was looking forward to the holiday."

"Might there have been some trouble at school that he feared would be reported?"

"No; his teacher was here Friday; we thought of that, as we did of everything, and wondered if she had sent a note home. But she said she hadn't, and, in fact, said he was doing better than he had ever done before."

"Was he hypersensitive? Did he brood over injuries?"

"He was just the opposite. If he felt wronged he let you know it, and everything was out and over within five minutes. He was patient and gentle, too, and when his little sister, who is 8, and loved to tease him, would exasperate him beyond endurance, he would hug her till she begged him to let go and promised not to do it again. The next time he would say, 'I'll slap you.' But she knew he wouldn't."

"Was he dealt with sternly?"

"He was dealt with firmly; he knew he must be obedient, but he was made to obey through love and kindness."

-cont

"Did he have all the freedom and play he wanted? Was he allowed to bring boys in to play with him?"

"It is one of our boasts," said Miss McCormick, sincerely, "that this is a home, not a house. There is no part of it kept shut off for visitors. The children could come in the drawing room or the playroom. Willie often came in here"—looking around the well-furnished reception room—"especially when there were gentlemen here who knew anything about baseball. He was just getting old enough to enjoy it and liked to talk with big men who knew something of it. Down in the playroom there were always children from the neighborhood. They had gay frolics there, and out on the back lawn, where there's plenty of room for tennis and croquet and baseball. The night before his disappearance they had a gay time downstairs dancing a cakewalk and singing 'Dem Goo-Goo Eyes.'"

"Haven't you, during ten days, been able to think of any unpleasant incident previous to his disappearance?"

"Indeed I have not. We've talked that all over without result. And even if there had been, I assure you Willie McCormick would rather be whipped than go out in the dark alone."

"Was he inclined to be reticent?"

"No; he never could keep a secret. If he had been planning any such escapade he would have told somebody, probably his sister Gertrude. There was a wonderful affection between those two. Being two years older, she assumed a sort of motherly attitude toward him. If anyone said anything against Willie she was up in arms in a moment, defending him and pleading for him. She would sacrifice herself to shield him. And if she saw him getting the worst of a game in the street, such as marbles, she'd make up some excuse to get him in. If Willie had intended running away he couldn't have kept it from Gertrude, and he wouldn't have gone without kissing her good-by. The following day we made the children go to school, but Gertrude refused to go into the classroom and stayed in the playground all day. There couldn't have been a household where the loss of a child could be felt more keenly."

Mrs. McCormick turned her face away. She was the only one left in the parlor. One by one the family had slipped away, unable to control their grief.

*-cont*

### Sister Alone Has Borne the Strain.

"I am the only one who has been able to keep up," she said, "and I realize some one must try to be calm and cheer the others. Margaret kept up until Friday; then she broke down. On that night Willies used to sleep with her because the sister he slept with attended a society meeting and didn't get home until late. He used to wash his hands and face till they shone, then hold up his hands and say: 'Now, Miss Margaret, am I sweet and clean?' and invariably his pains won him a kiss. Margaret was brave until Fridy night; then she went all to pieces."

"Was Willie careful in his attire, or was he shiftless, after the manner of ten-year-old boys?"

"He was one of the most particular little fellows I ever saw. He was as dainty as a girl. There's another reason why being a tramp would never appeal to him. You couldn't induce him to wear a collar the second day, and he'd have his morning bath if it made him late to school. He liked cleanliness and comforts and goodies too well to risk doing without them.

"Another thing he liked was his air rifle. Now, if a boy had a wild desire to run away and shoot Indians, as some one has suggested, he'd take his rifle with him and he would also provide himself with funds, which he read'ly could have done. He had just one cent which mother had given him, and the only toy he had was a wooden whistle, which all boys around here have to play wtih.

"Was he affectionate?"

"Oh, yes; we all are. We were a very happy family, and, most of all, the children were taught to love and reverence their mother. Willie realized that if he hurt his mother's feelings or worried her it would give her as much pain as if he struck her. So how could the runaway theory be true, when he knows it would break her heart to be without him for a day?

"Why, I never saw such suffering as his mother has gone through. The only moments when, from sheer exhaustion, she has fallen asleep, she has dreadful nightmares and has seen his face, distorted with suffering and tearstained. When it gets to be 2 or 3 o'clock, and mother thinks everyone is asleep, she slips out of bed to pray and watch by the window. If some definite information does not come pretty soon, there is no telling what tragedy the outcome will be. The letters, which are the work of fiends, have put us all into a frenzy, regardless of our resolution not to believe them.

*Cont'*

"Some of the threats are too horrible for publication. One of them was to cut off the boy's ears and send them by mail. The following morning mother received a large mail. The first letter she opened was from my aunt, inclosing a rare specimen of seaweed. Mother did not wait to see what it was. She fell swooning into our arms.

"Can you imagine anyone so depraved as to perpetrate this thing? Is it not worse than murder? Why, it is slow murder for us all. And yet if our boy were brought back to us, safe and sound, it seems as if I could almost forgive the pitiless wretches who have tortured us."

The strange disappearance has had no parallel in this part of the country since little Marion Clarke was stolen and hidden in the Pocono mountains.

Willie was a wideawake little chap of 10, the only boy in a large family, the pet of his parents and his big sisters. His father was reported to be worth considerable money until his death two years ago.

The family lives on Ogden avenue in a large, old-fashioned frame house surrounded by shade trees and a spacious lawn. The interior decorations give evidence of good taste and refinement. Some of the near neighbors are welthy. A person not familiar with Mr. McCormick's business affairs would judge from appearances that he had plenty of money.

Willie disappeared during the evening of Wednesday, March 27. He had arranged to go to church with two of his sisters. It was about 7:15 p. m. when they helped him on with his overcoat and started. Willie told the mto go slow and he would overtake them as he wished to run down stairs and get his cap. He left the house about three minutes later.

### *The Chicago Tribune April 22, 1901*

William McCormick, the boy's father, said tonight that he is convinced more than ever that his boy was kidnaped. Mr. McCormick would like to know what became of the Italian who worked on an unfinished house across the street from their home. Some of the boys in the neighborhood used to annoy the Italian, and the day before Willie McCormick disappeared he chased Willie and three of his companions, but did not catch them.

Mr. McCormick went to Mr. Jones, the contractor, and asked him for the Italian's name, but Jones said he did not keep the names of his men.

Willie disappeared during the evening of Wednesday, March 27. He had arranged to go to church with two of his sisters. It was about 7:15 p. m. when they helped him on with his overcoat and started. Willie told them to go slow and he would overtake them, as he wished to run down-stairs and get his cap. He left the house about three minutes later.

Mrs. Tierney, who lives three or four doors from the McCormicks, says that Willie came to her gate after leaving his house and asked her if her little son Lonnie could go with him to church. Mrs. Tierney told him no—that Lonnie had to take his music lesson.

Willie was seen again during the next fifteen minutes by a Mr. McMurray. He was still on Eaton avenue, about 100 yards from his own gate, but in an opposite direction from the church.

"He was talking with a larger boy as I came along," said Mr. McMurray. "Willie stood out in the street facing the boy, who was at the edge of the curb. They were near an electric light and I saw his face plainly. The other boy's back was turned and I did not recognize him."

## Cont-Chicago Tribune April 22, 1901

### Seen by Friends Later.

Tommy Black, a companion of Willie and of about the same age, states positively that he saw Willie about 8 o'clock that same evening leaning against the fence on the street corner by the church. Tommy had been to the barber's and was on the opposite side of the street. He says he did not say anything to Willie and that the latter said nothing to him.

There are some persons who think Tommy is mistaken, but he says he is positive. None of the church-goers remembers seeing him, and no one has been found who saw him afterward.

The people in Highbridge who knew Willie are almost unanimous in the belief that he was kidnaped. Their strongest argument is that he was afraid of the dark. Members of his family say that he could not be induced to go anywhere alone after dark, and that at night time he insisted on having an open door between his bedroom and that of his sisters. Mrs. Tierney tells how Willie came to her house one night recently to borrow some playing cards and insisted on her coming out to the steps and watching to see that he got safely to his own home. Lonnie Tierney, Tommy Black, and a dozen other boys tell of his fear.

These small apartment buildings were built across the street from McCormick's home in 1901 by the contractor JH Jones.

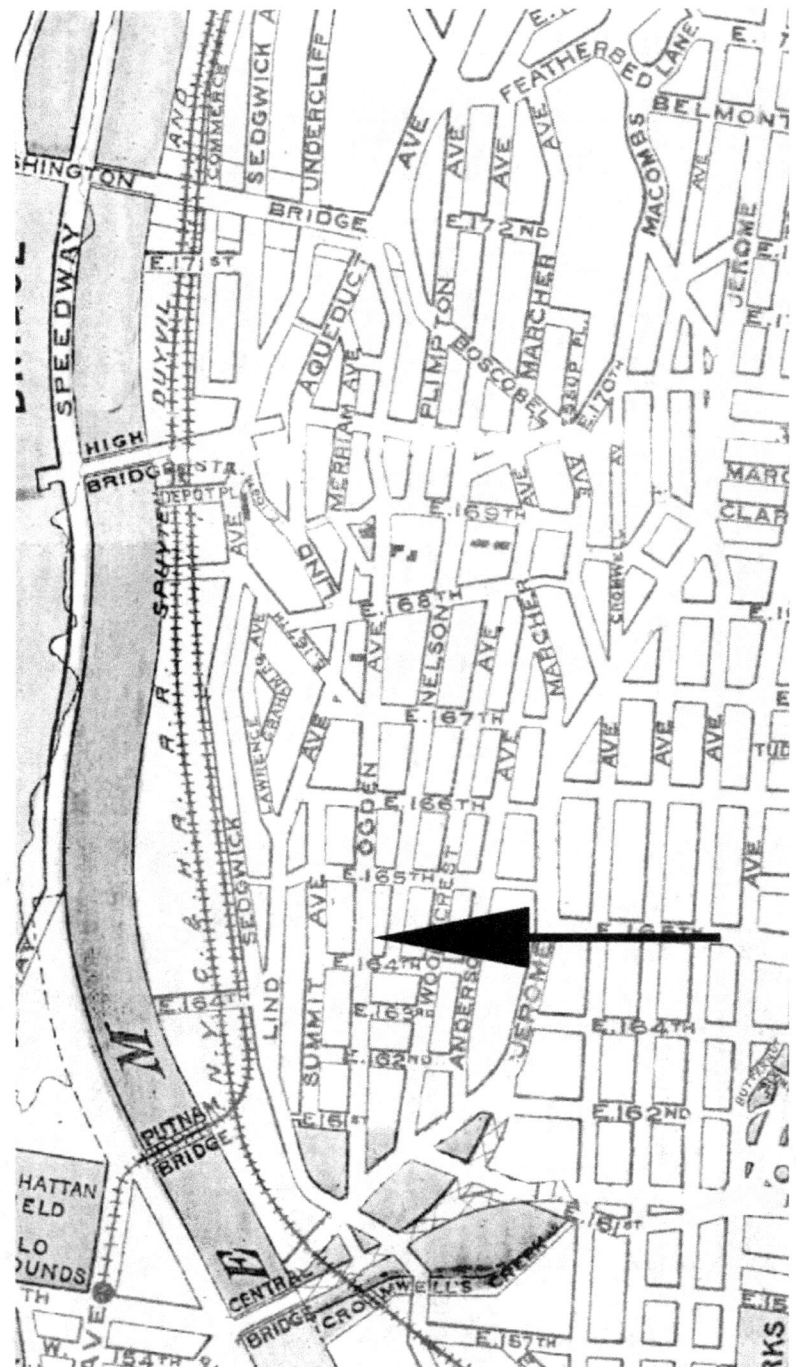

**The Point of Arrow indicates the 4 small apartment buildings constructed by contractor JH Jones in 1901. (They are still there and fully occupied as of 2022)**

### The Baltimore Sun April 23, 1901

**VIRGINIA GIRL MADE OFFER**

**Miss Mullin's Sympathies Were Aroused By McCormick Case.**

[Special Dispatch to the Baltimore Sun.]

NEW YORK, April 22.—It was Miss Mary Mullin, the young niece of the Rev. James A. Mullin, pastor of the Church of the Sacred Heart, in Highbridge, who recently offered, through the clergyman, the reward of $10,000 for the return of the missing Willie McCormick and the capture of his kidnappers. In her sympathy Miss Mullin voluntarily offered a large part of her private fortune to hasten the quest for the boy.

Miss Mullin was born in Virginia and was educated in convents in Montreal and in this city.

The information in this section of the 1900 Federal Census is interesting.

It shows that James Mullins arrived in the USA in 1855. It also shows his brother's daughter, Mamie, who grew up in Virginia was living with him in the Bronx in 1900.

This apparently insignificant tidbit of information was not readily available to the police in 1901. However, today, with all kinds of public records available to the public, some folks believe the investigators of 1901 left far too many stones unturned.

Is it possible that the investigators did not look into Father Mullins' background?

The primary reason this information is significant is that it shows her father was born in Ireland. And why is that significant? Father Mullins reports that he was born in Ireland. Yet, several other Federal Censuses show multiple discrepancies in the records. The Federal Censuses from 1840, 1850, and 1860 show James being raised in the same close-knit family. One unproven theory is that James Mullins fled to Ireland at the start of the American Civil War and returned in the early 1870s as a Priest, having been Ordained a Priest in Ireland.

## The Owensboro Messenger April 24, 1901

### SHEEDY SEEKS STOLEN BOY.

**Noted Gambler Offers $5,000 Reward for Willie McCormick's Return.**

Buffalo, April 23.—Pat Sheedy, bland and serene, came to this city today with Mrs. Sheedy and took apartments at the Iroquois preparatory to moving into the residence in Porter avenue which he will occupy during the exposition.

The cosmopolitan gambler is going to try to recover Willie McCormick, who was kidnaped at Highbridge, N. Y., about three weeks ago. Today Sheedy made public the following offer:

"This is to say that I am empowered to pay $5,000 for information that will result in restoring Willie McCormick to his parents. I will give my word of honor that all dealings to this end will be strictly confidential and in good faith. The money will be paid by me personally when I am enabled to deliver the boy. I have accepted this commission on the condition that no person shall be harmed."

"PAT SHEEDY."

"I am ready to pay the $5,000 at the snap of a finger if I get the boy," said Sheedy, "but I must have the boy first. There can be no impression picture business, no leave-the-money-under-a-bridge, no burn-a-red-white-and-blue signal-and-walk-a-mile-backward. I keep my promise whether I make it to a kidnaper or to a clergyman."

### PERHAPS WILLIE McCORMICK.

**Boy Found at Stamford, Conn, Who Closely Resembles the Youth Said to Have Been Kidnapped.**

STAMFORD, Conn, April 25—Constables Schlechtweg and Oesinger of this city have found a boy here who resembles Willie McCormick of New York, who mysteriously disappeared from his home several weeks ago. They have communicated with the New York authorities, and a detective from that city is expected here late this afternoon.

According to the officers, the boy, who gives his name as Russell Waldron, arrived here about two weeks ago, and has been living with a well-known woman since that time. He has told several different stories.

*Boston Globe April 25, 1901*

## The Portsmouth Journal April 25, 1901

### NEW M'CORMICK STORY.

**Boy Said to Have Tried to Escape From a Gypsy Coach.**

New Brunswick, N. J., April 24.—Yesterday afternoon Harry Coulon of 114 Redmond street, Frank Dowdell of 42 Bishop street and Frank Boulger of 84 Burnet street were walking along Burnet street when they saw some gypsies approaching in a coach. A long haired man was driving, and two women were in the coach with a boy, who had a school uniform on.

"Betcher that's Willie McCormick, the kidnaped kid," said one boy to another.

"Hello, McCormick!" shouted one of the boys.

The boy in the coach, the three lads say, upon the mention of the name tried to get out of the coach, but the women pulled him back. The driver went on.

Chief of Police Harding was informed and telephoned to nearby places to pick the boy up on suspicion. The gypsies have not been located.

## The New York Tribune April 26, 1901

### THINK THEY HAVE FOUND M'CORMICK.

#### WOMAN SAYS HE IS BEGGING IN HARLEM— A GERMANTOWN FARMER'S CLEW.

A letter received on Wednesday night by Father Mullin, of the Church of the Sacred Heart, Highbridge, from Charles Deschamp, sexton of the Church of St. Vincent de Paul, in West Twenty-third-st., has been sent to Captain Titus, of the Detective Bureau, and is now being investigated by his men. In the letter the writer says:

A woman came into the sacristy of St. Vincent de Paul's Church and asked me to let you know that the McCormick boy can be found in St. Nicholas-ave., between One-hundred-and-forty-fifth and One-hundred-and-forty-sixth sts., where he is begging twice a week. He lives far uptown, with two other boys, so the woman said. She refused to give her name and address.

The father of the missing boy was visited yesterday by C. A. Rockefeller, of Germantown, N. Y., who said that a boy answering the description of the missing lad was employed on a farm near his home. Rockefeller was shown clothing similar to that worn by Willie McCormick when he disappeared, and is almost positive that the boy working on the farm is McCormick.

Rockefeller will have a photograph of the boy taken and sent to the McCormick family. A boy found at Stamford, Conn., was reported to be the missing one, but detectives from this city found such not to be the case.

## New York Times April 26, 1901

### Missing Boy "Clue" at Stamford, Conn.

STAMFORD, Conn., April 25.—Constables Schlechtweg and Oesinger of this city have found a boy who resembles Willie McCormick of New York, who mysteriously disappeared from his home several weeks ago. They have communicated with the New York authorities, and a detective from that city is expected here late this afternoon. According to the officers, the boy, who gives his name as Russell Waldron, arrived here about two weeks ago. He has told several different stories.

*The Democrat & Chronicle April 27, 1901*

# CLUE TO THE KIDNAPPERS

## DETECTIVE ON TRACK OF WILLIE McCORMICK.

## GYPSIES ARE SUSPECTED

## PAPER FOUND ON THEM BELONGING TO MISSING BOY.

## TWO GIRLS ARRESTED

**Members of a Band of Russian Gypsies in Camp Near Washington Found With a Scrap of Paper on Which Was Written the McCormick Girl's Name.**

Special Dispatch to Democrat and Chronicle.

Washington, April 26.—Detective Sergeant O'Connell, of New York, came to Washington to-night pursuing what is thought to be a hot clew in the McCormick kidnapping case.

## Cont'

The possession of a scrap of paper of the exact kind in use in the McCormick home at High Bridge, on which was written the word "Gertrude," the name of the sister of Willie McCormick, has been acknowledged by two Russian gypsy girls, members of a band in camp near Washington.

The girls, Hannah and Lizzie Michel, aged 16 and 14, respectively, were arrested this morning to await the arrival of Detective O'Connell. The story connecting them with the scrap of paper came from a local photographer, M. Kets Kemethy. Several days ago, he says, the gypsy girls came to his studio in Pennsylvania and left behind them the scrap of paper. Upon reading a newspaper article on the McCormick case, in which Gertrude McCormick's name was mentioned, Kemethy says he was struck by the coincidence, and thinking he had found a valuable clew, forwarded the paper, which he rescued from his waste basket, to the New York police.

With the aid of an interpreter, Detective O'Connell and a local detective questioned the gypsy girls two hours tonight. The girls admitted having had the scrap of paper, but said they found it. Questioning failed to shake this declaration. The girls said they had never been in New York. M. G. McCormick, of this city, who has offered $5,000 reward for the recovery of his nephew, was present during the detectives' interview and said he was convinced the gypsies knew more than they had told.

The theory is that the scrap of paper with Gertrude McCormick's given name on it, and, as it is said, in her handwriting, was on Willie McCormick's person when he disappeared. The arrest of the gypsy girls has created great excitement in the gypsy camp, and several of the band thronged the house of detention while the inquisition was on.

## *The Saint Louis Republic* April 28, 1901, Missouri

# NEW CLEW IN McCORMICK CASE MAKES IT PUZZLING.

## Photographer Turns Over to Police a Slip of Paper on Which Is Name of Willie's Sister, "Gertrude."

## GYPSIES GAVE IT TO HIM.

REPUBLIC SPECIAL

New York, April 27.—Captain Titus was, Friday, informed by the police of Washington, D. C., that they had in custody Hannah and Lizzie Michel, members of a band of gypsies, who were encamped at Highbridge, this city, a short time ago, on suspicion of being implicated in the kidnaping of Willie McCormick. One of the girls, it is said, while in a photograph gallery, dropped a piece of paper bearing the name of the missing boy. Captain Titus sent Detective P. J. O'Connell to Washington to make an investigation.

Confirmation of the importance of the clew was received in a dispatch from Washington. The paper contained the name "Gertrude," the significance of which was not understood by a Russian gypsy girl, who had it in her possession and whose curiosity caused her to ask a photographer of that city what it meant.

The photographer, M. Kemetzky, who is also a Russian, retained the slip of paper, and, having read that the name of Willie McCormick's sister was Gertrude, he sent it to the family. The result was the arrest Friday at a gypsy camp near Jackson City, Va., of Hannah and Lizzie Michel, 16 and 14 years old, respectively, and their examination Friday night by Detective O'Connell and M. G. McCormick, uncle of the missing boy.

### "Best Clew Yet Struck."

O'Connell declined to make any statement regarding the information obtained by the examination, but McCormick said:

"All I will say is that this is the best clew we have yet struck. That slip of paper was in the possession of Willie McCormick."

Where is the boy has not yet been established, nor have the detectives been able thoroughly to satisfy themselves about the manner in which the slip of paper came into the possession of the gypsy girls.

The photographer obtained the slip of paper from Hannah Michel last Friday. He says that she came to him and asked him to tell her what was on the slip, as she could not read English. He kept the paper, and on Sunday last read in a New York paper that a sister of Willie McCormick was named Gertrude.

### Question That Puzzles the Police.

For some reason, known only to himself, he decided that the name "Gertrude" had something to do with the McCormick case, and sent the slip to the McCormick family by mail. The family were astonished to find that the writing on the slip was that of Gertrude McCormick, and Willie's sister positively identified it as being a slip from a pad which she had used at her home on the evening Willie disappeared.

The New York detectives notified the Washington authorities, and Friday morning the photographer, accompanied by six detectives, went to the gypsy camp, where they arrested the two young girls.

The photographer identified Hannah as the girl who gave him the slip of paper. She denied at first having done so, but later admitted that he spoke truthfully, and explained that she had found the paper on the street near the bazaar here.

The detectives regard it as somewhat extraordinary that Mr. Kemetzky, the photographer, should have assumed that the name written on the slip of paper had any connection with the famous kidnaping case and as still more extraordinary that the name should turn out to have been written by the sister of the McCormick boy.

## The Chicago Tribune April 28, 1901

**Gypsy Girls May Give Clew to Missing Boy.**

Detective O'Connell of Captain Titus' staff, who went to Washington to follow up a clew to the missing boy, Willie McCormick, made a long report by telephone to Captain Titus tonight. He informed the head of of the Detective bureau that the gypsy girls, Hannah and Lizzie Michel, who were arrested in Washington on Friday had been sent to the House of Detention.

O'Connell said that a piece of paper with the name "Gertrude" written on it was given by the girls to a Hungarian photographer with whom they talked. It is claimed that this piece of paper was sent to the McCormicks and the name declared to be in the handwriting of Gertrude McCormick, the sister of Willie McCormick.

The girl could not remember when she had written the name, but was sure it was her handwriting.

*The Spokesman Review April 28, 1901*

## CLUE TO WILLIE M'CORMICK.

### Detectives Believe They Are on Trail of Missing Boy.

NEW YORK, April 27.—Captain Titus of the detective department held a conversation over the long distance telephone today with Detective McConnell, who is in Washington, on what is thought to be the most important clue to the missing Willie McCormick of High Bridge that has been unearthed. Captain Titus said today that the signature "Gertrude," found in the slip of paper that had been left at a photographer's in Washington by the two gypsy girls arrested there yesterday, had been compared with the signatures of Gertrude McCormick, the missing boy's sister, and that the two are almost identical. Captain Titus said he attached great significance to this clue and now had hopes of finding the boy.

### Gypsy Girls Released.

WASHINGTON, April 27.—The two gypsy girls, Hannah and Lizzie Michel, who were arrested here yesterday in connection with the disappearance of Willie McCormick, the New York boy supposed to have been kidnaped, were released from custody today, the police not being able to make a case against them.

## *The New York Tribune August 28, 1901*

### WORKING ON GYPSY CLEW.

#### DETECTIVE FOLLOWS M'CORMICK THREAD IN A BIG ENCAMPMENT IN ALEXANDRIA—PHOTOGRAPHER'S ACTION.

A gypsy camp at Alexandria, Va., is the point at which the Police Department is at present lending its energy in the search for missing Willie McCormick. Detective O'Connell spent all day yesterday investigating the camp. Early last evening he made a long report by telephone from Washington to Captain Titus. He was ordered to return to Alexandria to resume the search.

In his report to Captain Titus the detective said that he went to Alexandria, and there found a big gypsy encampment, just outside of the town. In it are three tribes. Each of the tribes has a camp of its own.

"When I arrived at the encampment," said Detective O'Connell. "I made inquiries regarding the boys there, and learned that there was only one. He is a lad about seven years of age. I found one man that could speak passably fair English. He is an uncle of the Michel girls who at present are detained by the Washington police. I learned that the tribes in camp at Alexandria were three of five tribes which had migrated to this country from Russia. The three tribes here arrived in this country about five months ago. The other two tribes left Russia two years ago.

"My informant told me that the tribes at Alexandria arrived at Nova Scotia five months ago. They travelled through a portion of Canada overland, and finally reached Portland, Me. They then moved to Boston. At that place all of the male members of the tribes applied for citizenship papers. After staying in Boston a few days the tribes went to Philadelphia by boat. My informant says that none of the members of the tribes stopped in New-York.

### -con't The New York Tribune August 28, 1901

"The camp at Alexandria was established nearly three months ago. Since coming here the tribes have not moved at all. The person from whom I got my information vehemently denies that any of the members visited New-York. He says that it is the intention to hold a reunion of all of the five tribes in the near future."

O'Connell said that the Michel girls were not released from custody by the Washington officials, but were sent to the House of Detention.

O'Connell questioned the photographer who received the "Gertrude" paper from the two gypsy girls. The photographer is M. Ketz Kemethy, a Hungarian. His place is at No. 1,109 Pennsylvania-ave. One of the girls, Kemethy declares, gave him a paper on which was written the name Gertrude. She asked Kemethy what the writing on the paper was. He told her, and retained the paper. Kemethy says that a few days later he was reading a New-York paper. An editorial regarding the McCormick kidnapping case caught his eye. Kemethy asserts that he saw the name Gertrude in the editorial. He wrote to the McCormicks and inclosed the slips of paper.

Asked regarding this piece of paper, Captain Titus said last night that it was a rough piece of white paper, about 5 inches long by 2½ or 3 inches wide. On one side of the paper, in a schoolgirl hand, was written the name Gertrude. The writing was identical with that of Gertrude McCormick, the sister of the missing boy. Miss McCormick had seen the writing on the paper, and she unhesitatingly asserts that it is hers. She cannot remember, however, when and under what circumstances the name was written.

Captain Titus says that he watched the newspapers closely regarding the McCormick case, and he does not remember having seen the name of Willie McCormick's sister, Gertrude, printed. He thinks it a most significant fact that Kemethy should have known the name. The letter and the "Gertrude" paper have been sent to Washington.

Mr. McCormick, the father of the missing boy, at his home last night, said, regarding the slip with the name Gertrude written on it: "I showed the slip to my daughter without letting her know where I got it, and asked her whose writing it was. She replied: 'That is my writing, papa.' I then got my daughter to write her name on another piece of paper. When compared the two writings were identical. I believe that this is an excellent clew and think it will lead to the recovery of my boy."

# Gypsies

For more than 500 years there have been stories circulating in Europe and Eur-Asia about Gypsies and other ethnic and religious minorities kidnapping children. And yes, even in the USA, during the 19th and 20th Centuries, there have been hundreds of news articles in small towns and large cities about Gypsie Families and Clans being the first suspects in kidnapping cases.

Old customs & myths die hard. It's an age-old folk tale: "Watch your kids around the Gypsies, or they'll steal them."

And, as with most earlier cases in the USA and Europe of missing children, newspapers were eager to increase their circulation by unscrupulously printing false stories about Gypsies, also known as the Roma People.

However, the Gypsies were not always the target of false kidnapping stories.

Jewish people were also falsely targeted and labeled as "Children Snatchers."

For centuries, Jews were subject to the *Blood Libel Legend*, which claims that they kidnap and murder Christian children in secret ritualistic sacrifices. The Blood Libel legend, though now largely but not entirely erased from common beliefs. Yet for some, it is still in the collective minds of those who refuse to accept the truth.

## New York Tribune April 29, 1901

## STILL WILLING TO PAY.

### FATHER MULLIN PRACTICALLY RENEWS HIS OFFER OF A REWARD FOR RETURN OF M'CORMICK BOY.

Little progress was made in the McCormick case yesterday, although the police of this city and of Washington were active. Captain Titus told about the failure of another clew. A penholder was sent to Captain Titus from Washington by Detective O'Connell. The holder was partly made of cork, and part of it was painted green. One of the gypsy women who have been detained by the Washington police said she had found it with the piece of paper bearing Gertrude McCormick's name. It was thought that possibly the penholder had been taken from the McCormick home by the kidnappers. The McCormicks, however, said that they had never seen such a penholder in their home.

Detective O'Connell telephoned to Captain Titus late yesterday afternoon. He said that he and Detectives Weiden and Palmer, of the Washington police, had been to Alexandria, where the gypsies are, but had obtained little information. They found no one who had seen a boy who might be McCormick. They learned that there are three gypsy camps in the northeastern suburbs of Wash-

## -cont New York Tribune April 29, 1901

ington, and O'Connell said these camps would be visited to-day.

O'Connell said that it was his intention to visit a house in Virginia-ave., Washington. Two women who live in Maryland-ave. had informed the police that they had seen a boy who resembled young McCormick in the Virginia-ave. house.

Mr. McCormick, the father of the missing boy, said yesterday that he was convinced that some one was detaining the boy in or near Washington. Mr. McCormick had a fright Saturday night which resulted in a severe attack of heart trouble. After supper he sent his three little children to the barber shop near the house to have their hair cut. When they came home they ran quickly up the steps. Mr. McCormick, who was sitting in the parlor, thought he heard the voice of the missing boy, and ran to the door, thinking his son had finally come home. The disappointment was keen when he found that his ears had deceived him, and he fainted. It was several hours before he regained his usual composure.

Father Mullin referred to the McCormick case in the course of his remarks at the 8 o'clock mass yesterday morning. He said that since his school had been closed by order of the Board of Health he had missed the bright and happy faces of the children, of whom he was so fond, and then he added: "If I feel this way about children who are not of my flesh and blood, what must be the condition of mind of a parent whose son has been stolen and who cannot learn with what fate he has met?"

Father Mullin said that while he had been compelled to withdraw his offer of a $10,000 reward for the return of the missing boy and the arrest of his kidnappers, on account of the annoyance it had caused him, if the boy was returned to his parents and his kidnappers apprehended he was still willing to pay the $10,000.

## *The Star Dispatch April 29, 1901*

**POLICE WITHOUT CLUE**

No Developments of Importance Concerning Willie McCormick.

**DISAPPEARANCE STILL A MYSTERY**

Father of the Boy Ill at His New York Home.

VIEWS OF DETECTIVES

Little Willie McCormick, who is supposed to have been kidnaped near his father's home at High Bridge, N. Y., the 27th of last month, has not yet been found. The investigation of a supposed clue found here ten days ago in the recovery of a piece of paper alleged to have been in the McCormick house, has not yet been fully abandoned, so far as Detective O'Connell of New York is concerned. Detectives Weedon and Parham of the local force, who were detailed to assist the New York detective have, however, about given up hope of accomplishing anything in the case. Detective O'Connell has made several reports over the long-distance telephone wire to Capt. Titus, chief of New York detectives. The slip of paper on which was written "Gertrude," the name of the missing boy's sister, has been sent to New York, together with a penholder that was wrapped in the slip of paper at the time the latter was left at the photograph gallery of M. Kets Kemethy. One of the gypsy girls stated she picked up the piece of paper in question near a horse bazaar and used it to wrap the pen in. What part the pen is alleged to play in the disappearance of Willie McCormick is not known, but the local police infer that a similar holder was stolen from the McCormick home. Where the pretty gypsy maiden actually got the penholder is not known, for the company has probably manufactured millions of that particular pattern. It is known that the girl got such a penholder from the business office of The Star about ten days ago. She was in the office making an effort to induce the clerks to give up coin. She spied the penholder, asked for it and it was given her. The holder is an olive green one, with a cork finger rest, and in it was a Spencerian pen.

## –con't Star Dispatch April 29, 1901

**Nothing of Importance Develops.**

Hannah and Lizzie Michel, the gypsy girls who were released Saturday morning, went to the camp. The detectives visited the camp, but learned nothing of any importance. They also visited Alexandria and other places, but no trace of the missing boy was found.

Yesterday the gypsies broke camp, drove through the city and recrossed the river at the Chain bridge, and camped a short distance from the bridge last night. They stated to the detectives that they were going to Richmond. The two police experiences here were enough for them. The queen of the tribe announced Saturday that Washington was a bad place, and they would not come here again.

Saturday afternoon the police received information that a boy, possibly Willie McCormick, was living on Virginia avenue. This boy, it was claimed, ran away from his home and came here. The detectives learned that he had been here since early in March, and also that he was several years older than the McCormick boy.

Capt. Titus of the New York detective bureau, in an interview yesterday, is reported to have said:

"I have learned by experience how unreliable is the testimony of a child of Gertrude McCormick's age. A child may mean to tell the truth, but its memory is uncertain and its mind is led unconsciously by that of an older person. Gertrude McCormick says positively that the handwriting on the scrap found by the gypsy girls was hers. I would not place any great reliance upon this statement if it had not been supported by comparing her handwriting with that found upon the scrap.

## *con't Star Dispatch April 29, 1901*

**Much Requiring Explanation.**

"If we assume that the paper which the gypsy girls say they found in the horse market in Washington was taken from the McCormick home there is a great deal back of this case which must yet be explained. It must have been something more than chance which prompted the gypsy girls to take it to the photographer, and which impelled him, after retaining it for three or four days, to forward it to the McCormick family. I am not satisfied with his explanation. Why should any one place any value upon such a scrap? There was absolutely nothing in it to suggest the missing boy, except that it bore the name Gertrude, which is his sister's name.

"When my men went to the gypsy camp to inquire about the girls arrested they found their mother and an uncle. Nothing was said at the outset about the missing father. We now believe that such a person exists, and that he left the camp, according to his friends, three or four weeks ago. We have been unable to fix the time definitely.

Concerning the father of the girls, their mother explained to a Star reporter, as heretofore stated, that she had left him, but when she would not say. Capt. Titus, it is reported, ascertained that John Michel, the father, disappeared about a month ago, and the New York detectives will make every effort to find him.

**Catholic Pastor Refers to Case.**

The prolonged disappearance of the boy was spoken of by the Rev. Father Mullin in the Sacred Heart Church at High Bridge yesterday.

## con't Star Dispatch April 29, 1901

"I want to explain my position in this matter," said Father Mullin. "It has been said that I was harsh in my discipline of Willie McCormick and other boys who were taking instructions. I want to deny this. I never made a threat to Willie McCormick that would cause him to fear me. I have never said that Willie McCormick was a bad boy. He was the average ten-year-old boy, brisk and full of life.

"I want us to have a special prayer here this morning for the return of Willie McCormick to his distressed parents and sisters. Let us pray earnestly for this. I want to say further that it was cabled to Rome that Willie McCormick was missing from his home and that he was probably kidnaped and the entire church all over the world will pray for his return. It is known in Rome that I offered $10,000 for the return of the boy and the capture of the kidnapers. That action will be approved.

"While I withdrew my reward temporarily because of the hordes of mountebanks, clairvoyants, fakirs and fortune tellers who came to see me, there is not a member of my congregation but knows that if the boy should be returned tomorrow and the kidnapers brought to justice Father Mullin would be ready to pay $10,000 and probably more. I miss Willie McCormick from the church. He was a good boy. Let us pray specially now for his return to his heartbroken parents."

*—con't. Star Dispatch April 29, 1901*

**Father of the Boy Ill.**

William C. McCormick, father of the boy, is ill. He is suffering from a nervous attack. Yesterday his condition was made more serious when he heard what he thought was the voice of his missing son, and then found that he was mistaken. In his explanation concerning the paper on which the name of his daughter was written Mr. McCormick said:

"The letter and slip with the name Gertrude written on it are genuine all right. They were sent to me by a Washington photographer. The slip with the name on it was inclosed in the letter, and the writer of the letter said that ne had received the slip in a very mysterious manner. Further than this there was no explanation.

"I showed the slip to my daughter without letting her know where I got it, and asked her whose writing it was. She replied:

"'That is my writing, papa.'

"'Are you very sure of it?' I asked my daughter.

"'Certain,' she replied.

"I then got her to write her name on another piece of paper. When compared the two writings were identical. I believe that this is an excellent clue, and think it will lead to the recovery of my boy.'

**Possible Mistake.**

"If the paper recovered from the photographer was genuine," said a member of the police department today, "somebody has made a mistake. Certainly, if the paper has been traced to the McCormick home the gypsies should be detained until a more complete investigation could be made."

There was no protest entered by the New York detectives against the release of the Michel girls, nor was there any warrant sworn out upon which they could be held for the New York authorities.

*Buffalo Evening News April 30, 1901*

## TOUCHING APPEAL TO MISSING BOY.

### Father Mullin Acts on the Possibility That McCormick Boy Ran Away.

(From Yesterday's Last Edition.)
(By Associated Press.)

NEW YORK, April 29.—Father Mullin said this afternoon that the statement made by him asking Willie McCormick to come home under his protection and without fear if he had run away and not been kidnaped, was to cover any possible chance that the boy had run away and was afraid to return home. The statement is as follows:

"To Willie McCormick: If you are alive, sick or well, write to me or send some word that your parents may be spared from insanity or perhaps death. You will not be punished. I, as your father in the church, promise that you will be given back to the arms of your family, and that not one breath of reproach will reach you.

"Your poor mother is on the verge of insanity; the physicians fear also for her life. Your father is fast losing his memory, and his hearing is affected from constant anxiety caused by your continued absence from home.

"If you are afraid of your parents' anger, come to me. Your protection shall be absolute.

"(Signed.) REV. J. A. MULLIN."

## The Helena Independent April 30, 1901

### Pat Sheedy, Professional Gambler.

#### TRUSTED BY HONEST MEN AND THIEVES.

While the New York police are sleeping over the case of Willie McCormick, kidnapped more than two months ago, Pat Sheedy comes forward with an offer for the missing boy. Since Sheedy is known to every sport in the United States, and to most other men who keep track of what goes on, the following dispatch is interesting:

New York, April 19.—Capt. of Police Titus declared to-day that he is not paying any attention to the offer of Pat Sheedy to give $5,000 and ask no questions if the missing boy, Willie McCormick, is sent home. "Sheedy is not authorized to act for us," added Capt. Titus, "and I'm not taking any notice of him or his reward. We have something else to do here besides noticing fakes and fakers."

What right has Police Captain Titus to call Pat Sheedy a faker?

Willie McCormick disappeared from his home in New York two months ago, and the circumstances surrounding the case pointed to kidnapping. Letters received by the family since then strengthen this theory. Whether it was the work of some one animated by personal hatred or a seeker after money is not known. McCormick, the father, is a well-to-do contractor and has wealthy brothers.

The boy's family, the New York police, friends of the family and private detectives have been searching high and low for the child ever since he went away, without finding one tangible clue to his whereabouts. They have been spurred on by the offer of $2,000 in rewards, $1,000 by the father and $1,000 by the uncles.

Now the mother, turned gray by grief, is on the verge of insanity. The physicians have said that to save her the boy must be brought back, no matter how. Thus it is that the family, disregarding the police and other searchers, determined a day or two ago to treat with the criminals, if, as it is believed, criminals are at the bottom of the affair, and pay what they might demand, in whatever form it might be demanded, and under whatever conditions they might select.

#### CRIMINALS SCARED.

Then it was that the family was confronted with a great problem. So great has been the hue and cry for the boy that the criminal or criminals would never rely on any assurances or promises of immunity and reward held out by the family, the police or a private detective agency.

A man nor set of men facing 20 years imprisonment, would be exceedingly wary in dealing with any of the above named. How were they to know it was not a trap to ensnare them? What reason had they to believe that the moment their hand was disclosed it would not mean immediate arrest? What code of morals requires honesty or sincerity in dealing with a thief?

It therefore became necessary to find an anomaly of a man to act as a go-between. The right man must be one to whom a large sum of money might be entrusted with the knowledge that he could be depended upon to act honestly towards the family and the community, and at the same time have the confidence of the kidnappers. They must feel that they could trust him implicitly and confidently place their liberty in his hands.

#### PAT SHEEDY THE MAN.

The man was found and thus it came that this notice has been scattered broadcast:

"New York, April 17, 1901. "Notice to Whom It May Concern:

## -con't The Helena Independent April 30, 1901

"This is to say that I am empowered to pay $5,000 for information that will result in restoring Willie McCormick to his parents. I give my word of honor that all dealings to this end will be treated as strictly confidential and in good faith.

"The money will be paid by me personally when I am enabled to deliver the boy. I have accepted this commission on the condition that no person shall be harmed. P. F. SHEEDY."

Who is this P. F. Sheedy," on whom both thieves and honest men rely? What manner of man is he?

Any gambler or sporting man in Europe or America will answer. He is Pat Sheedy, a gambler, a man who has made his livelihood by his wits and skill at cards. That is Pat Sheedy. There must be something to justify the universal confidence in the man.

Gamblers will tell you what that something is. They say it is because he is a "man on the level." Translated that means he is a man of his word, dealing honestly, according to his standard, with every one he meets; never treacherous and devoid of duplicity.

### A FINE LOOKING MAN.

Pat Sheedy is 50 or 60 years of age, a tall, heavy-set man, with gray hair, a smooth-shaven face and with the cold blue eye characteristic of the gambler of sensational literature. He is always fashionably, though not flashily, dressed, wears little or no jewelry, and when engaged at his avocation, either as banker or player, his face is as impassive as moulded bronze. With his friends in his hours of relaxation his eyes light up, his laughter is frequent and anecdotes of his world-wide experience flow from him.

Born in Ireland, Sheedy came to this country in his early youth. It has been said that he came of a fine family, and that he was intended for the priesthood. He is well educated, and speaks French almost as well as English.

He was known as a gambler many years ago, and has conducted gambling establishments in the west, in New York, Saratoga, Boston, Newport, Paris, France, and Cairo, Egypt. Incidentally he has staked his money at faro in all the great gambling centers. He has been worth $500,000 and has been down to borrowing car fare. He has had a royal palace for his gambling house and has put up with a little back room behind double locked doors in a side street when the police were momentarily expected.

Once he published a newspaper. That was for revenge. He tells about it. It was in Hartford, Conn.

### BARRED BY OTHER GAMBLERS.

"I wanted to open up there," he says, "and the local gamblers standing with the authorities shut me out. I bought an evening paper to get even with the authorities. It cost me $25,000 before I sold out and I was shot at twice, but I ran two of the men I was after out of town. Then I left."

During all this time his reputation for squareness grew. It was all based on a peculiar standard of morals of his own. He originated a code of morals for himself. This was briefly: "It is all right to do things when you are doing business, but when you pass your word to a friend, keep it."

Thus it was that the bankers and thieves, business men and confidence men began to trust the man. And thus it was that he gained friends in all ranks. This redounded to his profit, for it became a familiar experience to him to gamble for some man willing to risk money, but without sufficient confidence to play himself. Many a night behind Sheedy's chair in New York gambling houses wealthy men of almost every walk of life have stood breathless, watching the gambler hazard large sums of money on the turn

### con't The Helena Independent April 30, 1901

of the cards. The money belonged to the men behind the chair. If Sheedy won, the gains were divided; if he lost there was the experience for those who had advanced the money. In addition, the loser had the comforting thought that he had lost honestly. He was willing to trust the player again and again.

This confidence has been illustrated in other ways. There was one time in Boston when Sheedy had met with a streak of hard luck and found himself one morning after a 24-hour bout with the "tiger" absolutely penniless. It was necessary for him to obtain money to get to New York. While he was meditating he noticed that he stood in front of a bank. After a little more reflection he entered and asked to see the president. He was shown into a room occupied by a busy, curt old man, who snapped out: "Well, what is it?"

"I would like to borrow $1,000," said Sheedy.

"What's your security?"

"My word!"

The banker wheeled around in his chair to look at this strange visitor. He thought of cranks.

"Can't negotiate that here," he said, grimly. "Good morning."

"Wait a moment!" interrupted the gambler. And then he spoke for a minute or two—mentioned some names and recalled some incidents.

"Oh!" exclaimed the banker. "I have heard of you."

Then he wrote out his personal check for the amount asked.

The money was returned two days later.

## FOR A GAMBLING PALACE.

Another time, and this was perhaps the most striking incident of Sheedy's career, he wanted to establish a great gambling house at Cairo. He had a royal palace in his mind, the rent for which was $40,000 a year, besides which it would be necessary for him to give two concerts a week to the aristocracy and nobility, and also to serve champagne free. He had $40,000 at the time and needed more. He went to a prominent business man in New York and spoke of the project.

"You can have $25,000 from me," was the quick answer. Another man added a like sum, and the gambler went to the Orient with nearly $250,000 in gold. He conducted the place for three years. Every man who had befriended him got his money back with interest, and when Sheedy closed the establishment last year he had plenty of money. But he will not reopen this spring. He says the price demanded for protection, even in the shadows of the pyramids, is excessive.

That illustrates the confidence in which respectable men hold him. The incident of the Gainsborough portrait

*con't The Helena Independent April 30, 1901*

shows the other side. The painting was cut from its frame 35 years ago, and in that time the police had never gained a trace of it. It was worth a fortune. J. P. Morgan has offered the owners $125,000 for it. In all these years the portrait was lying in the false bottom of a trunk in a Chicago warehouse. The thieves were afraid to produce it, for that meant instant detection, and they could not claim the reward offered. Several months ago one of them asked Sheedy to find out how much would be given if the picture were returned safely. Sheedy did so with the express understanding that no search would ever be instituted for the thieves. The owners sent him $10,000, and one of them came to this country. Sheedy paid over the money, and to whom he paid it or where will never be known.

A PLUCKY MAN IS SHEEDY.

He also has nerve. That is illustrated not only when he was conducting his Hartford newspaper, but by an incident of his career when he was manager for John Sullivan. The latter had in moments of alcoholic enthusiasm sent several managers to hospitals with broken limbs and bruised bodies.

Soon after Sheedy entered into business relations with the then champion of the world the giant started for the gambler intending to throw him out of a window. He never arrived, for he found himself looking down the muzzle of a revolver and listening to a voice saying, coldly:

"Don't try it on, John. You won't be able to finish." After that Sheedy was able to do more with the fighter than any other man.

So that is the man whom the McCormicks have asked to help in restoring their child—a man with whom the kidnappers, it is believed, will willingly enter into negotiations. He has accepted the mission, and has passed his word that he alone will know the secret of the crime. No one who has ever known him doubts this for a moment, and he says simply:

"It's a long chance, but I'll take it for the sake of the mother."

He is waiting at the Sturtevant house in New York to hear from the under world.

## *Altoona Tribune* April 30, 1901

### An Appeal to Willie McCormick.

NEW YORK, April 29.—Father Mullin said to-day that the statement made by him asking Willie McCormick to come home under his protection, and without fear if he had run away and not been kidnaped, was to cover every possible chance that the boy had run away and was afraid to return home. The statement is as follows:

"To Willie McCormick: If you are alive, sick or well, write to me or send some word that your parents may be spared from insanity and probably death. You will not be punished. I, as your father in the church, promise that you will be given back to the arms of your family, and that not one breath of reproach will reach you. Your poor mother is on the verge of insanity; the physicians also fear for her life. Your father is fast losing his memory and his hearing is affected from the constant anxiety caused by your continued absence from home.

"If you are afraid of your parents' anger, come to me. Your protection shall be absolute.

[Signed] "REV. J. A. MULLIN."

## *The Evening World* April 30, 1901

# $18,000 FOR BOY.

### Joseph Hennessy Adds $2,000 to the Sum Already Offered for Willie McCormick.

Two thousand dollars additional reward for the safe return of Willie McCormick or the capture of his kidnappers was proffered to-day by Joseph R. Hennessy, of One Hundred and Seventy-seventh street and Third avenue.

Mr. Hennessy is a restaurateur. Three weeks ago kidnappers attempted to chloroform and has been abduct his favorite nephew, Clifford Fountain, a lad of four years, who lives with his parents at No. 1048 Park avenue.

Mr. Hennessy has been greatly incensed and has been urging the police on in their efforts to run down the perpetrators of that attempted crime.

The incident made him strongly conscious of the suffering of the McCormick family, and he offered the additional reward to-day in the hope that the money would keep alive interest in the case and prove a final incentive to the return of the boy.

Mr. Hennessy says his reward is without condition. He will place the money in the hands of "Pat" Sheedy, to be added to the $5,000 reward already given by Mr. Michael McCormick.

If the kidnappers are caught the money will be paid over to those instrumental in their capture.

"I would give more if I could afford it," said Mr. Hennessy. "If the boy is alive it is high time for his abductors to give him up. If he is dead it is about time that those who had to do with death should be captured and punished."

Up to date $18,000 in rewards have been offered for the return of the McCormick boy.

The Standard Union May 1, 1901

# MISSING BOY'S CHUM FOUND

## Joseph Garland May Know Willie McCormick's Hiding Place— Talk of More Kidnaping.

One of missing Willie McCormick's playmates, Joseph Garland, a runaway boy, has been captured on a farm near Brewsters, N. Y., and the police believe he can give a clew to young McCormick's whereabouts. Garland lived at North Haven, and disappeared at the same time as did McCormick, for whose return an aditional reward of $2,000 has been offered by Joseph R. Hennessy, a restaurant proprietor at 177th street and Third avenue, in the Bronx.

The McCormick family has received a letter saying that three other Highbridge families are to suffer from the kidnapers, and that two boys and a girl are to be carried off. Mrs. Margaret Sanders, of 2713 Boulevard, Manhattan, called at the McCormick home, last night, and said that Willie is on a farm between New York and Ossining (formerly Sing Sing), but would not reveal the source of her alleged information.

*The Standard Union May 1, 1901*

## ONLY A SCRAP OF PAPER.

### It Forms a Clew, However, in the Hunt for Missing Willie McCormick, of High Bridge.

New York, April 27.—Captain of Detectives Titus held a conversation over the long distance telephone with Detective McConnville, of the central office, who is in Washington, following what is thought to be the most important clew in regard to the missing William McCormick, of High Bridge, that has yet been unearthed.

Capt. Titus said that the signature "Gertrude," found on the slip of paper that had been left at the photographer's in Washington by the two gypsy girls arrested there, Friday, had been compared with the signatures of Gertrude McCormick, the missing boy's sister, and the two are almost identical. Capt. Titus said he attached great significance to this clew, and now had hopes of finding the boy.

*The Standard Union May 1, 1901*

# OFFER $18,000 FOR STOLEN BOY

## Whoever Finds Willie McCormick Will Get a Small Fortune

Eighteen thousand dollars in cash now awaits the lucky person who will return Willie McCormick safe and sound to his parents.

Father Mullin, of Sacred Heart Church, Highbridge, to-day renewed his $10,000 reward and announced that he was at last inclined to accept the theory that the boy had been kidnapped.

The rewards now offered for the boy, who has been missing from his home since March 27, are as follows:

| | |
|---|---|
| Oscar Willgerodt | $1,000 |
| Michael McCormick | 5,000 |
| Rev. J. J. Mullin | 10,000 |
| Joseph R. Hennessy | 2,000 |
| Total | $18,000 |

All of these rewards are offered unconditionally, with no questions asked. If the kidnappers give up the boy, they will get the money. If any one gives up the kidnappers, the rewards of Father Mullin and Mr. Hennessy will be turned over to them.

## The Evening World May 1, 1901

Since Willie McCormick disappeared Father Mullin has been firm in the belief that the lad ran away. He questioned his schoolmates and Sunday school chums, and what he learned from them convinced him that Willie was not the little angel he had been painted by doting parents and loving sisters.

The fact that he believed him a runaway did not deter the priest, some weeks ago, from offering $10,000 reward to any one who would restore the boy to his grief-stricken family. Later Father Mullin announced he had withdrawn the reward, as he was pestered by clairvoyants and silly people who took up his time with their theories of how the boy might be found.

"I have spent all my spare time on this case," said Father Mullin to-day. "I went entirely on the theory that the boy had run away and was not far away. I have personally investigated many clues along that line. Yesterday I started out early and went systematically over Brooklyn and to every ferry line along the East and North River.

"When I returned last night I talked the case over with Judge Tierney and I confess that I am now inclined to accept the kidnapping theory. For that reason I have decided to renew my reward."

## New York Tribune May 1, 1901

**UNCLE OF A LAD WHO WAS CHLOROFORMED IN ATTEMPTED KIDNAPPING OFFERS $2,000 ADDITIONAL.**

Two thousand dollars more reward has been offered for the safe return of Willie McCormick to his parents. The offer has been made by Joseph R. Hennessey, proprietor of a restaurant at One-hundred-and-seventy-seventh-st. and Third-ave. He has not deposited the money with any one, but says his offer is good, and that he will pay the money if the boy is found.

Hennessey's nephew, Clifford Fountain, four years old, was chloroformed and an attempt made to kidnap him three weeks ago in Park-ave. The attempt was frustrated.

## The Dayton Daily News May 2, 1901

# ANOTHER CLEW IS EXPLODED

### In the Mysterious Willie McCormick Kidnaping Case—Gypsies Driven Out

WASHINGTON, May 2.—The Washington clew in the Willie McCormick alleged kidnaping case is about exploded. The detectives have practically concluded that the slip of paper and the mysterious coincidence by which it came into their possession were the result of connivance between parties in New York who had access to the McCormick home and others. The Gypsies who figured so largely in the matter have been driven from Alexandria county and now are on their way to Pittsburg.

*The Marion Star May 2, 1901*

## NINE THOUSAND.

### That Many Dollars Will Be Paid for Return of McCormick Boy.

New York, May 2.—A reward of $9,000 and no questions asked is now offered for the safe return of 10-year-old Willie McCormick, who disappeared from his home March 27. An uncle of the boy offers $6,000, a neighbor of the McCormicks $1,000 and now Jos. R. Hennessy, a restaurant keeper, has added $2,000 to the fund.

Hennessy was influenced in making the offer by the fact, he says, that an attempt was recently made to chloroform and kidnap his nephew.

Rev. Father Mullan offered $10,000 for the return of the boy and conviction of the kidnapers, but was so pestered by cranks he withdrew it. While the formal offer was withdrawn Father Mullin has said he will pay the money anyway if the child stealers are convicted. No reward has been offered by the city.

*The Buffalo Commercial May 2, 1901*

## M'CORMICK CLUE COLLAPSED.

Washington, May 2.—The Washington clue in the Willie McCormick alleged kidnaping case is about exploded. The detectives have practically concluded that the slip of paper and the mysterious coincident by which it came into their possession were the result of connivance between parties in New York who had access to the McCormick home and others. The gypsies who figured so largely in the matter have been driven from Alexandria county, and are now on their way to Pittsburg.

*The New York Times May 3, 1901*

## WANTS McCORMICK REWARD.

### A Woman's Visit to a Restaurant Keeper Who Offered $2,000 for Missing Boy's Return.

Joseph Hennessy, the restaurant keeper of 4,215 Third Avenue, who, a few days ago offered an additional reward of $2,000 and no questions asked for the return of lost Willie McCormick of Ogden Avenue, High Bridge, yesterday received a call from a woman about fifty years old, who asked him for the money. He asked her for the boy, and she told him that she would produce him. She declined to give her name or say where she lived, except that it was in Park Avenue. Mr. Hennessy soon dismissed her, with very little idea that anything will come of her visit.

Before the woman left, however, she told one of the waiters that she would bring the boy to the restaurant this morning.

Father Mullen of High Bridge, who also offered a ten-thousand-dollar reward for the boy, which he afterward withdrew, received an anonymous letter from Brooklyn yesterday stating that the writer had seen the boy in a restaurant at Third Avenue and One Hundred and Twenty-seventh Street Wednesday night. There is no restaurant that would accord with a description given near that corner.

*Salina Daily Republican Journal May 4, 1901*

## RUMOR OF WILLIE McCORMICK.

### Reported That He is in a Woman's Hands, Held For Revenge.

By Scripps-McRae Press Association.

Chattanooga, Tenn., May 4—Detective Maingault of Kentucky claims that Willie McCormick, kidnapped in New York, is in Chattanooga with a certain woman. He says the boy was taken because the father's testimony sent the woman's sweetheart to prison years ago. The police are investigating.

**The Marion Star May 4, 1901**

Chattanooga, Tenn.—The chief of police of this city received a letter Friday from Captain G. F. Titus of the New York Detective bureau, inclosing a letter from Wm. M. Maingault of Uniontown, Kentucky, stating that Joseph Fibley of Chattanooga claims to know all about the kidnaping of Willie McCormick. Maingault's letter was written to Rev. J. A. Mullin. A search is being made for Fibley.

## The Nebraska State Journal May 5, 1901

### HAS TRACE OF THE KIDNAPER.

#### Abductor of McCormick Boy Said to Be at Chattanooga.

CHATTANOOGA, Tenn., May 4.—The McCormick kidnaping case that has stirred up the city of New York equally as much as the Cudahy kidnaping did Omaha, has assumed a local tinge. A detective named Maingault, living in Uniontown, Ky., claims that the kidnaper of young McCormick is in Chattanooga, and that his name is Joseph Fibley. He has written a letter containing this information to Rev. J. A. Mullin, of the church of which the McCormick family belongs. This letter Father Mullin turned over to Capt. George F. Titus of the New York detective bureau, which is working on the case.

Capt. Titus sent the letter to Chief Hill, asking him to investigate. The letter arrived this morning and is as follows:

"UNIONTOWN, Ky., April 22.—To Rev. J. A. Mullin, New York: Dear Sir: I have one Joseph Fibley in Chattanooga, Tenn., who claims to know all about the kidnaping of a small boy that belongs to your church, named Willie McCormick. On account of bad cut on right arm he requested me to write letter today to one Pat Sheedy,

*—con't The Nebraska State Journal May 5, 1901*

advising him to keep still and say nothing. He says that Sheedy is an officer and knows where he is. He claims that a woman named Mrs. Jennie Hickman has the boy at her house, detained there for safe-keeping. He also claims the boy's father to be poor and that he did steal him for money, but because his father's evidence sent him to prison in his past life for four years. He says that Sheedy and the police are trying to make money. That you know very well, he says, there is $6,000 reward offered for them, which I think a shame for any officers to act in such a matter.

"I will be able to send you his written statement in his own handwriting, should you think there is anything in it. I believe it to be true, if anything of the kind has happened. If you or any of the parties that may be interested in such a case will send me $75 expense money, and a written contract agreeing to pay me $6 per day and expenses, I am able to run down the parties in a few days. It will save that large reward. It will cost me $75 to make the trip from here to Chattanooga and thence to your town with him.

"You may send warrants of arrest for one Joseph Fibley. I herewith enclose old letters for reference to my standing, showing my credit with parties with whom I have been engaged. I will hold Fibley in sight until I hear from you. Please write me fully.

(Signed)
"WILLIAM W. MAINGAULT.
"Box 36, Uniontown, Ky., Rep. Amn. Detcy. Agency."

Chattanoogo detectives are at work on the case.

## *The Gazette (York, PA.) May 6, 1901*

**Sheedy, Who Holds the $5,000.**

Pat Sheedy, who is called "the prince of gamblers" because of his reputation for square dealing and generosity and also because he is a regular Beau Brummel in the matter of dress, has lately appeared in a new role. He was selected by Michael McCormick as the custodian of the $5,000 reward to be paid for the return of the missing 12-year-old boy Willie McCormick of New

PAT SHEEDY.

York. The police of New York were a little stirred up because Sheedy announced that the money would be paid "and no questions asked" for the boy's return. Michael McCormick, who lives in Washington, is Willie's uncle.

## *The Evening Times* May 7, 1901

### THE MISSING M'CORMICK BOY.

**Captain Titus, of the New York Detectives, Makes a Statement.**

NEW YORK, May 7.—Captain Titus, of the headquarters detective bureau, made a statement today concerning the supposed kidnapping of Willie McCormick. "The boys' father," said the captain, "comes down here almost daily with letters from gypsies, clairvoyants, and strangers of every description, offering suggestions as to the boys' whereabouts. I receive letters of the same sort. Wherever there is the possibility of a clue amounting to something I have had my men investigate.

"We are beginning to believe that the boy was drowned or else was taken away on shipboard. There is one thing more we are about to do, and that it to open the plug of a sewer in the neighborhood of the McCormick home. The detectives will be on hand to help in a careful search, and if there is a body there we are going to find it."

## *Alexandria Gazette* May 7, 1901

In New York today Captain Titus said that his men had exhausted every clue to find Willie McCormick, and he had given up hope of finding the boy alive. He believes that the boy has been drowned.

## The Evening World May 7, 1901

Six weeks ago to-morrow, at 7.30 in the evening, Willie McCormick and his two young sisters were in the front hall of their home, in lonely, well-shaded Ogden avenue, Highbridge. They were setting out for an evening meeting at the church, several blocks away, down the avenue and across some vacant lots.

*A MYSTERY OF THE GREAT CITY.*

"I've left my cap downstairs in the dining-room," exclaimed the boy. "Go ahead and I'll catch up with you."

As they were late the sisters walked rapidly, thinking that their ten-year-old brother would overtake them quickly by running. But he did not. And since they saw him hurry away to go down to the basement dining-room he has not been seen.

There is no longer the slightest doubt that he was kidnapped. The probabilities are that he was seized before he reached the end of the fence along the front of the McCormick place and that his sisters were not more than 300 feet ahead when the men took him.

The police have searched. Rewards aggregating $16,000 have been offered. Immunity has been offered the kidnappers. All in vain. No trace. No clue. No hope.

Was he taken to some lonely house not far away? Was he taken to a boat on the Harlem near by, and is he held there while the boat skulks along the coast from one secluded inlet to another? Was he put aboard a coasting or sea-going schooner?

Is he dead? Or are the kidnappers waiting until the public has forgotten so that they may deal directly with the agonized parents without fear?

There is not the sound of footsteps in Ogden avenue coming toward that home, there is not the rattle of wheels in that quiet street, but that the mother and sisters start up and rush to the front windows. And every night the women of that household—the mother and sisters—lie awake painting on the black curtains of the darkness the horrors that may have overtaken the little boy.

*LISTENING FOR THE STEP THAT COMES NOT.*

This is a world of sorrow and suffering. Its deepest anguish is for those who wait in uncertainty for a lost one whose fate is uncertain. And of that deepest anguish the deepest depth is for those whose lost one is a child, so timid, so sensitive, so helplessly dependent upon love and care.

## The New York Tribune May 8, 1901

### WELL SEARCHED FOR M'CORMICK BOY.

#### CAPTAIN TITUS HAS GIVEN UP HOPE OF FINDING HIM ALIVE—WILL LOOK IN SEWER.

Captain Chapman, of the Highbridge station, yesterday afternoon searched an abandoned well at One-hundred-and-sixty-third-st. and Ogden-ave. in an effort to get some trace of Willie McCormick. Captain Titus, of the Detective Bureau, has given up hope of finding the boy alive, and thinks he has been drowned in the river or in a sewer.

The sewer near the McCormick home, at Ogden-ave. and One-hundred-and-sixty-fifth-st., will be searched probably some time to-day for the boy's body, which Captain Titus thinks may be in there.

## The Dayton Herald May 9, 1901

### POLICE BELIEVE HE HAS BEEN DROWNED

#### Captain Titus Has Given Up All Hope of Finding Willie McCormick.

New York, May 9.—Captain Titus, of the Detective Bureau, has no hope of finding Willie McCormick, the missing High Bridge boy. Every clew possible has been followed, and Titus thinks the boy has been drowned, although there is a chance he was kidnaped and taken to sea.

Young McCormick disappeared from his home six weeks ago. At one time there were rewards amounting to $16,000 offered for his recovery, but they brought no results.

The Butte Daily Post May 10, 1901

## LONG SEARCH FOR WILLIE M'CORMICK IS ENDED.

Mystery of His Disappearance Cleared Up in His Death—Was Thought to Be Kidnaped.

New York, May 10.—The body of Willie McCormick, who disappeared from his home in this city some weeks ago, was found in Cromwell creek at 161st street and Railroad avenue. The body was identified by the boy's sister.

It had been supposed that the boy was kidnaped, and rewards aggregating $16,000 were offered for his return. The parents were poor people, and there could have been little hope of them paying any considerable amount. But the priest of the parish, much interested in the case, offered $10,000 for the boy's return, and others made up the balance. Many alleged clues were followed to disappointment. It was thought that he had been carried away by gypsies, a band of whom had been in the neighborhood.

## *The Dayton Herald May 10, 1901*

# BODY OF WILLIE M'CORMICK FOUND

**BULLETIN.**

New York, May 10.—The body of the missing ten year old boy, Willie McCormick, was found in Cromwell's Creek this afternoon.

His body was found at 2:30 o'clock this afternoon. The face of the dead boy was eaten away, and his sister identified him by his clothing.

Willie McCormick disappeared from his home about a month ago. Searching parties failed to locate him in the city, and his family believed him to have been kidnaped. Time elapsed, and many clues in different cities were run to earth. Rewards aggregating $16,000 were offered for his return. The police refused to believe that he was kidnaped, and expressed the opinion that he had been drowned in a sewer or in the river near his home. Detectives have been working continuously on the case.

## *The Brooklyn Citizen May 11, 1901*

**THE McCORMICK BOY.**

The discovery of the body of ten-year-old Willie McCormick, of High Bridge, in Cromwell's Creek, about a mile to the south, disposes of the kidnapping story which has been a part of the stock-in-trade of the sensational press ever since he disappeared on March 27th.

Every person of right feeling, while sympathizing with his family over the loss of the child's life, will be glad to know that at last the suspense and uncertainty, more dreadful in effect than the truth, are now ended; and though sensationalism is still striving to maintain its influence on curious minds by hinting at signs of foul play, the parents at least will probably pay no further heed to the effort.

They know the worst, and, bad as that is, it is in the nature of things that it should bring some relief to souls distracted by vague doubts and fears aroused by each fresh tale of clews here and signs there indicating that the boy was either murdered by kidnappers who dared not claim the ransom or was being held for a greater offer.

As matter of fact, from time immemorial boys have disappeared from home all over the world; some were drowned and never found; some went to sea and never returned, while others did, and some started for the West to scalp Indians and were glad to be yanked out of a hiding place by the police within forty-eight hours with their own scalps where Nature placed them. And in none of these cases of late has there been much said about them, until the kidnapping of the Cudahy boy in Nebraska gave the cue to the sensation mongers which has been made such use of in the McCormick case.

## The Buffalo Evening News May 11, 1901

### WILLIE M'CORMICK DROWNED.

The body of little Willie McCormick was found yesterday afternoon by two young men who were fishing near the New York Central railroad bridge in a shallow stream known as Cromwell creek, almost a quarter of a mile from the boy's home. This is a melancholy ending of the search for the boy who was thought to have been kidnaped. The little boy must have wandered off to play at the river's edge or to view the passing current from the bridge and fallen into the stream, whose waters have hidden him from sight for the past six weeks.

Mr. McCormick, the father of the dead boy, still thinks the letters he received just after his son disappeared were written by people who kidnaped him. A Coroner's investigation will determine if death was caused by accidental drowning and relieve the doubt thus expressed by Mr. McCormick.

The sympathy of the whole country has been aroused in this case, and large sums of money have been offered to reward those who could give information concerning the boy. It is a sad gratification to the parents to realize the truth of the mysterious disappearance of their son and know where he rests in peace.

## *The Star-Gazette May 11, 1901*

# WILLIE M'CORMICK

## His Body Found in Cromwell's Creek.

## NEAR BOY'S HOME.

## Not Yet Definitely Known How Missing Child Came to His Death.

New York, May 11.—There is mystery no longer as to the whereabouts of "Willie" McCormick, ten years old, who disappeared six weeks ago last Wednesday.

## Cont'

His dead body yesterday afternoon was found floating in Cromwell's Creek less than five blocks from his home in Ogden avenue, High Bridge. There is no explanation as to how the little fellow lost his life in the offshoot of the Harlem river, and whether or not he was alive when the body entered the water can only be determined after an autopsy by a coroner's physician.

It was when hopes of ever learning of the missing boy's whereabouts had about been dispelled when the police and citizens in every part of the country had bent every energy, and fruitlessly, to restore Willie McCormick to his heart broken and distressed parents and sisters, that the little fellow's body, fully clad, but bearing the evidence of having been in the water for several weeks, was found floating on the surface of Cromwell's Creek.

Those who lifted the lifeless little form to a pier suspected that it was that of Willie McCormick, who disappeared on March 27, when he had left home to go to the Church of the Sacred Heart for the evening service, but it was not until the boy's father, William, and a daughter, Carmelita, had looked upon the body and identified it that at least part of the Willie McCormick mystery was at last solved.

## *Cont'*

Willie McCormick's body was taken to the desolate home, in Ogden avenue and Kemp place, last night, where a distracted mother and father, with their ten daughters—for it must be remembered that Willie was the only boy in the family—gazed tearfully at the features of him who had been accounted among the missing for so many weeks. There was belief among those of the family that Willie's death was still unexplained.

Willie's father and mother, and those sisters old enough to reason, remembered that a few days after Willie disappeared letters were received signed "Kidnapped" and "Kidnapper," in which a ransom of $200 and then $2,000 was demanded. One letter in particular stated that the latter and larger amount was to be deposited at a certain place under the Central, or McComb's Bridge. Strangely significant was the fact that the boy's body was found close by the spot where the ransom was to have been left.

While thinking of that the McCormick family thought, too, of the first supposed clue they had that Willie had been foully dealt with by one of the workmen who was employed about the cellar and grounds of a house being erected in Ogden avenue directly opposite the McCormick home.

On the very day that Willie disappeared it was known that he, with other boys, his playmates, had annoyed one of the workmen, and that one of these more initiated than the others, had not only chased Willie in the morning while the boy was on his way to school, but had lain in wait for the boy at noon time when he returned home for luncheon.

*-cont'*

John Garfield, is the tender of a drawbridge over which the New York Central and Hudson River Railroad company's trains pass Cromwell's Creek, just below McComb's, or the Central Bridge. His attention was attracted to an object that was bobbing up and down in the creek about 2:30 o'clock yesterday afternoon. Garfield say that it was the clothed body of a boy floating face downward with both arms outstretched. At about the same time Robert Boyd and Isaac Wagner, of No. 644 East 156 street, two fishermen, had been the object and started to row toward it.

Garfield now summoned Policeman Charles Francis, of the West 152nd street station, and the police of the Morrisania station were notified to send a patrol wagon. Policeman Francis, with two men, entered a rowboat and towed the boy's body up Cromwell's Creek about five hundred feet, where it was lifted to the pier of a brick yard.

When the news that a body had been found reached the McCormick home both Mr. and Mrs. McCormick burst **into tears, while their daughter ran in** search of their wraps. Mr. McCormick, who several times during the absence of his boy had followed up false clues, put on his hat and coat and left the house with his daughter Carmelitor.

## Cont'

They hurried down the street to Jerome avenue and crossed a little wagon and trolley bridge to the brick yard. A small crowd had gathered around a little object on the pier. Approaching quietly the father and daughter and sister looked down upon the features of the loved one. Between their sobs and tears they recognized the clothing and a cent, a penknife, a metal advertising medal and a skate key.

Carmelita had to be supported by her father, and the kind hearted men who stood nearby. She had all but swooned. The identification has just been completed when a patrol wagon arrived from the Morrisania police station, and the body was borne away. Mr. McCormick and his daughter returned to their home as speedily as they could.

Willie McCormick's back was covered with mud. This indicated that the body had rested for some time in the bottom of some stream, whether it was the Harlem River or Cromwell's Creek. It was a matter that baffled all who were acquainted with the case to understand how the body had found its way into the creek. When Willie left home at a quarter after seven o'clock on Sunday night, March 27, to go to church he walked northward, for he was last seen by Mrs. Tierney at that hour, when he asked his playmate "Lorrie," her son, to accompany him to church, where he had promised to meet his little sisters Sadie and Gertrude.

*Cont.*

Willie was never seen at the little frame place of worship, which lies a third of a mile norheast of the McCormick home and is reached by a circuitous route. There was no reason for his going within a quarter of a mile of the creek. Where the body was found the water is twenty feet deep.

It was at first believed that "Willie" had fallen into the sewer, probably that on Jerome avenue, which enters into Harlem River. It is impossible, however, because of a grated door, for a body to emerge and be carried by the tide ito the creek. There is no question, therefore, but that "Willie" fell or was thrown into Cromwell's Creek, but what point could not even be conjectured.

There was no evidence that the body had been weighted, but to-day an examination by Coroner Lynch, in whose hands the case is, may bring out some developments.

*The Arkansas Gazette May 11, 1901*

NEW YORK—The body of Willie McCormick, who disappeared from his home in this city some weeks ago, was found in Cromwell creek, at One Hundred and Sixty-first street and Railroad avenue. The body was identified by the boy's sister.

*Buffalo Inquire May 11, 1901*

# WILLIE M'CORMICK'S BODY IS FOUND

### Boy Who Has Been Missing for Six Weeks.

## DROWNS IN A CREEK

### His Parents Believe His Death Was Due to Accident.

**Odd Circumstances Connected with the Boy's Disappearance—Rewards Offered and Great Search Made.**

Special Dispatch to The Inter Ocean.

NEW YORK, May 10.—The body of Willie McCormick, who disappeared from his home in this city some weeks ago, was found today in Cromwell creek at One Hundred and Sixty-First street and Railroad avenue. The body was identified by the boy's sister. The parents of the boy said tonight that they had abandoned the idea of foul play and that they believe the boy had been accidentally drowned.

Willie McCormick, who lived at High Bridge, started from his home early on the evening of his disappearance six weeks ago to attend church. On his road he vanished—there is no other way to describe it. The police, his schoolmates, all his friends and relatives, and the friends and relatives of his family scoured the country for miles about his home. Detectives have ransacked all of New York city from Gravesend to the Yonkers line. All the newspapers of the city, and of the entire country for that matter, have been ringing for weeks with the strange story of his disappearance. His picture and his description have been scattered broadcast, and rewards aggregating thousands of dollars have been offered for his return or for news that would lead to the discovery of his whereabouts.

### The Search for the Boy.

Detectives have gone here, there, and everywhere trailing clews that seemed promising at first, all of which ended in disappointment. Letters came from all parts of the country describing boys that more or less accurately corresponded with Willie's description. But in every instance the result was the same—only bitter disappointment to the unhappy parents. They at last settled down to a sort of dull despair in the conviction that the boy had been kidnaped and that the criminals who did the deed had become afraid to restore him, even with the incentive of a large reward.

### His Strange Disappearance.

An extraordinary feature of the McCormick case was the manner of the lad's disappearance. Not a member of the family knew when he left the house or by what door he went out. They merely remembered that after one of his sisters had helped him on with his overcoat he ran downstairs to a basement room to get his cap. From that moment not one of them saw him again.

It was about 4 o'clock when he got back from school. He found his father putting up fence posts in the garden back of the house. The father asked Willie to help him with the work, by holding the posts straight while he, the father, stamped in the dirt around them.

The boy was busy at this until 5:30, when he and his father went to the house to tidy themselves for dinner. After Willie had washed his hands and face his mother sent him to the corner grocery, which is rather farther than a short city block away, to get some milk. He went and was gone an unnecessarily long time—twenty minutes or half an hour. About this, however, there was no mystery. Willie McCormick was a 10-year-old boy, and as given to fun as boys usually are at that age. He simply was skylarking with some of his playmates. A neighbor, Mr. Frank Tierney, saw him at this and told him he had better hurry home with his milk or he would have a score to settle with his mother.

Evidently the boy was of the same opinion, for he quit his skylarking and hurried for home. Near his gate he met three more of his acquaintances—Harry Therritt, much older than Willie; Lawrence Tierney, and Adrian McCloud. To these boys Willie said he was going to church as soon as he had had his dinner, and he asked them to go with him. They all declined, for one reason or another. Then Willie went into the house.

This was about 6:30 o'clock. His parents and the other members of the family say that he was not scolded for being so long on his errand. He sat down to the table with the rest of the family and ate such a dinner as a growing boy, who has been to school, been playing, and been helping put in fence posts might be expected to eat. When dinner was over he set about getting ready for church. As he was about this he spoke the last words his mother was destined to hear him speak perhaps forever.

"It will be a bad Easter week for Mrs. Thompson, mamma," he said, "with little Tina lying dead there in the house."

Mrs. Thompson was a neighbor, whose 5-year-old child had just died. This had made a strong impression upon Willie McCormick. His mother made some appropriate reply, and the boy then called to his sister Anna and asked her to comb his hair. This Anna did, and Willie was quite minute and explicit in his directions as to how it was to be parted.

**Gets Ready for Church.**

These preparations were all made in the basement of the house. Upstairs, in the main entrance hall, the boy's sisters, Gertrude and Sadie, were impatiently waiting for him to go to church with them.

"Come, Willie, hurry up," Gertrude exclaimed as he at last came running upstairs into the hall. "Hurry up. It's late already and we must go."

Willie's overcoat was on a rack in the hall and his sister helped him on with it.

"There," he exclaimed, when he had got the coat on, "I've left my cap downstairs. Go on ahead. I'll run down and get it and catch up with you."

The little fellow started on a run for the back stairs. His sisters did not see him after that moment. They went on out the front door, down the flight of steps in the yard to the street and walked rapidly off in the direction of the church.

There is some uncertainty among the members of the family as to the exact hour that this departure of the two sisters and Willie's hasty run downstairs for his cap took place. Devotions in the church were due to begin at 7:30 and would not last more than half an hour, and as the two girls were only a very little late in arriving at the church, it is probable that the actual time when Willie McCormick disappeared was somewhere very close to 7:20 in the evening. It was the 27th of March, just about one hour after sunset, and consequently dark.

The family knows that Willie went to the dining-room from the absence of his cap, but his actual disappearance, the exact point where he vanished from all knowledge of the members of the family was at the head of the stairs leading down to the basement. So far as his father and mother and sisters are concerned, the earth to all intent and purposes swallowed the boy at that place and

**Search Begun at Once.**

From that moment began the long agony for that unhappy family, which has known no alleviation to this day. The entire neighborhood was searched. The neighbors were roused out of their beds and joined in the search. At 11:30 o'clock the case was reported to the police, and a general alarm was sent out. The next day began the false "clews" and the false identifications. Willie had been seen in Jerome avenue; he had been seen in half a dozen other places in the neighborhood. A minute search was made that day as far as One Hundred and Eighty-Eighth street.

Of alleged clews, which, when probed, proved to be worthless, there were several. And there have been the adventurers trying

## -cont.

to make money out of the family's grief. April 2 they received a letter threatening to burn Willie's eyes out unless a certain sum of money was left at a certain designated spot. A few days later a Brooklyn car conductor was sure he had seen and talked with Willie on his car at Coney Island. Then a boy was held at Red Bank until detectives and acquaintances of Willie went and found out that it was not Willie. And so it has gone, letters to this day coming in an unbroken stream and all of them leading to nothing. It was the fixed belief of the police and the fixed belief of Father Mullen for a time that the boy had run away. The police worked on that line alone.

Rewards of $6,000 had been offered for the return of the boy. Of this amount $1,000 was offered by a neighbor of the family, and $5,000 by M. G. McCormick, uncle of the boy. The rewards were offered with the condition, "no questions asked."

### The Clew from Washington.

M. G. McCormick lives in Washington, D. C. Recently while at the Hoffman house in this city he received a letter from Washington which hinted darkly at knowledge of Willie's whereabouts. Soon after a Washington photographer sent to Mr. McCormick a scrap of paper which he said he had got from a gypsy. On the paper—which was a bit of white wrapping paper—was written the name "Gertrude," the name of one of Willie McCormick's eleven sisters. He was the only boy in a family of twelve children.

Miss Gertrude McCormick and the rest of the family believed that the scrap of paper was genuine; that in some manner inscrutable to them it came from Willie, for Miss McCormick was sure she recognized the handwriting as her own. There was correspondence with the photographer who sent the bit of paper, but nothing came of it. If anything, the episode only cast a deeper shade of mystery over the entire dark situation.

When Willie McCormick disappeared he had, so far as his parents know, just 1 cent in money in his possession. His mother had given him that to buy candy with at the corner grocery on his way to church. He never bought the candy.

## New York Times May 12, 1901

# AUTOPSY ON McCORMICK BOY.

## Physician Thinks Death Was Accidental—The Father Not Convinced.

Despite the fact that there is no evidence of foul play in the case of Willie McCormick, whose body was found floating in the Harlem River Friday, the parents of the boy refuse to be reconciled to the theory that death was accidental.

Coroners' Physician Riegelman of the Borough of the Bronx performed the autopsy yesterday afternoon at the undertaking establishment on West One Hundred and Thirty-first Street, where the body was taken Friday night. When seen last evening Dr. Riegelman said that the body had evidently been in the water ever since the night the boy was first missed on March 27, and that he was of the opinion that the boy had fallen into the water and was drowned. He said that there was no evidence of injury on the body, but the body had been in the water so long that it was almost impossible to tell positively whether the boy was alive or dead when the body first entered the water. However, he had no suspicion of foul play.

Mr. McCormick, however, still believes that his son was the victim of foul play, and suggests that he might have been thrown or pushed overboard by somebody who had a grudge against him. Several weeks ago McCormick was of the opinion that the boy had been made away with by an Italian laborer who was working on stone foundations near the McCormick residence whom the boys annoyed greatly, and who was known to have threatened Willie with bodily harm.

Late yesterday afternoon the body was taken home and services will be held to-morrow morning in the Church of the Sacred Heart at High Bridge, of which the Rev. Father Mullen, who offered $10,000 reward for the safe return of the boy, is rector.

## Saint Paul Globe May 12, 1901

# MYSTERY OF A LOST CHILD

**REWARD OF $18,000 FOR RETURN OF WILLIE M'CORMICK FAILS OF RESULTS**

**WAS A CASE OF DROWNING**

Detectives and Cranks Alike Interested, but Not a Trace of the Boy Until His Body Was Found.

The dispatches from New York Friday contained news of the finding of the body of little Willie McCormick, who had been accidentally drowned. The discovery clears up what had been regarded as the most impenetrable kidnaping mystery in recent years. Willie McCormick was a son of William McCormick, a retired florist of High Bridge, one of Gotham's suburbs. William McCormick was ten years old, and on Wednesday night, March 27, dressed to go with his sisters to a festival in the Church of the Sacred Heart. His sisters were ready before he was and left the house, telling Willie to follow when he had finished dressing. This was 7:30 o'clock in the evening.

For three days the family searched for the boy and then notified the New York police of his absence. Detectives were set on the case, and in a few days hundreds of clues of the usual kind that develop in this sort of a case had been run down, without effect. Chief of Detectives Titus personally took up the matter and claimed to have discovered on one occasion that the little fellow was fond of horses and was ambitious to become a jockey. Brooklyn street car conductors were willing to swear they had carried him in the direction of Sheepshead Bay, and some of the touts around that neighborhood came to the front with the positive assertion that the boy had been seen loafing around the paddock. Grooms and wipers and jockeys and trainers told the police day after day that they had seen him, but he was elusive. Titus finally abandoned his theory and began to think that perhaps after all the boy had been stolen.

Gypsies and Italians were suspected. Two or three of the former were arrested. All the gypsies that had camped in Westchester county for a year or more were followed and their camp searched, but none of them had Willie McCormick.

Then the cranks took a hand in the matter and wrote letters to the heart-broken father and mother. Some of these letters were threatening, some insulting, some savored of blackmail and others were idiotic. The father decided to offer a reward of $1,000 for the return of his boy. This produced another letter, which demanded the money should be placed in an old boiler in the upper part of Third avenue. This was actually done, and two detectives carefully watched the spot for hours, but no one came near the sack of gold. Then Oscar Willgerodt, whose nephew was once kidnaped, added $1,000 to Mr. McCormick's reward. This was followed by an additional $4,000 offered by Michael McCormick, an uncle of the missing boy. Joseph R. Hennessy, a restaurant man, became interested in the case, and added $2,000. All of this had

## Con't Saint Paul Globe May 12, 1901

no effect, and then Father J. J. Mullin, of the Sacred Heart church, capped the climax by offering $10,000 reward for the missing boy. This made a total of $18,000.

One bright morning New York was startled by the announcement that Pat Sheedy, "honest gambler," had decided, after his success as a go-between in the restoring of the stolen Gainsborough, to restore Willie McCormick. He gave out signed statements, in which he announced he was prepared to take the money and find the boy. He sneered at the police and declared himself the only real detective in business in Gotham. Strange to say Mr. Sheedy's disinterested efforts did not meet with unanimous approval. First, one of the newspapers made a very harsh remark about Mr. Sheedy and then the police decided that they were perfectly able to do all the detecting needed around the city for quite a while yet. Mr. Sheedy took offense at the cold-blooded way in which his kind offers had been spurned and in a very dignified manner announced that he should retire from the case and compel the detectives to struggle along without his aid.

When little Willie disappeared Father Mullin was firm in his belief that the lad had run away. He questioned his school chums and Sunday school mates, and from what he learned was convinced that little Willie was not the angel he had been painted, but this did not deter the priest from offering the reward to anyone who would return the boy to his grief-stricken parents.

*-cont*

The latest in the strange case came from Chattanooga, Tenn., when William M. Maingault, a detective living in Uniontown, Ky., asserted that the kidnaper is Joseph Fibley, and is in Chattanooga. He has written a letter containing this information to Father Mullin. This letter Father Mullin turned over to Capt. Titus, who sent it to Chief of Police Hill, of Chattanooga, to investigate. In the matter the detective says:

"I have a man in Chattanooga, Tenn., who claims to know all about the kidnaping of a small boy that belongs to your church named Willie McCormick. On account of a bad cut on right arm he requested me to write a letter today to one Pat Sheedy advising him to keep still and say nothing. He says that Sheedy is an officer and knows where he is.

"He claims that a woman has the boy at her house, detained there for safekeeping. He also claims the boy's father to be poor, and that he did not steal him for money, but because his father's evidence sent him to prison in his past life for four years.

"If you or any of the parties that may be interested in such a case will send me $75 expense money and a written contract agreeing to pay me $6 per day and expenses. I am able to run down the parties in a few days."

Willie McCormick's father declared, however, that he had never testified in such a case as that mentioned in Detective Maingault's letter. He regards the letter as of no more importance than the very many others he has received from parts of the country.

### *The Chicago Tribune May 12, 1901*

Dr. John F. Riegelman, Coroner's physician in The Bronx, performed an autopsy today on the body of Willie McCormick, which was found in a creek near his home on Friday. "The boy's death was caused by drowning," said the Coroner's physician, "and I could find nothing in the case which would make it appear that he was murdered, as his relatives seem to think."

**Autopsy Shows Willie McCormick Was Drowned.**

Dr. Riegelman was of the opinion that the body had been in the water five or six weeks, and in all probability since the night the boy disappeared, March 27 last.

"I still believe my boy was murdered," said Mr. McCormick. "I have received information to the effect that on several occasions my boy was chased by an Italian whom he had teased. This Italian was a laborer, and I asked the police to find him, but they tell me that the Italian had nothing whatever to do with the case. My poor boy certainly was murdered."

The Rev. Father Mullen said the public had not been told that Willie McCormick was seen half an hour after he left home. He seemed in trouble. When boy friends hailed him he burst out crying and ran away.

A letter received at a newspaper office tonight said Willie had on two occasions been chased by an Italian. "Willie took the Italian's hat to tease him, and to get even the Italian threw Willie into the creek," the letter said. The letter was signed "M. F. Brown."

### *The Rochester Democrat & Chronicle May 12, 1901*

The mystery of the disappearance of "Willie" McCormick, the New York boy for whose discovery and return to his home a reward of $16,000 was offered, has been solved, as a special to this paper of yesterday showed, by the finding of his drowned body in a creek not far from the boy's home. Probably had there been less excitement over recent kidnappings a search for the boy's body would have been made in the water where it was found and all the trouble over the case would have been avoided.

## *The New York Sun* May 12, 1901

### SAYS SON WAS MURDERED,

#### BUT AUTOPSY REVEALS THAT WILLIE M'CORMICK WAS DROWNED.

**Story That the Boy Was Thrown Into the Water by an Italian Laborer Whom He Had Teased to Be Investigated by the Police—The Lad Was Seen Running Toward the Creek.**

Dr. John F. Riegelman, Coroner's Physician in The Bronx, performed an autopsy yesterday on the body of Willie McCormick, which was found in a creek near his home on Friday.

"The boy's death was caused by drowning," said the Coroner's physician, "and I could find nothing in the case that would make it appear that he was murdered, as his relatives seem to think. The only mark upon the body was one upon the left cheek, which was probably caused after death, when the body may have come in contact with some object in the water."

Dr. Riegelman was of the opinion that the body had been in the water five or six weeks, and in all probability since the night the boy disappeared, March 27 last.

"I still believe my boy was murdered," said Mr. McCormick, "and the fact that the autopsy shows that death was due to drowning does not do away with the belief held by me and my friends that Willie was murdered. I have received information to the effect that on several occasions my boy was chased by an Italian whom he had teased. This Italian was a laborer and I asked the police to find him, but they tell me that the Italian had nothing whatever to do with the case. My poor boy was certainly murdered, for he never could have fallen into that creek accidentally."

## -con't The New York Sun May 12, 1901

Detective Petrosini, the Italian sleuth of the Central Office, was detailed on the case yesterday for the purpose of running down this story. He reported to Capt. Titus last night that he could get no verification of the story. The Italian who was said to have figured in the case had left High Bridge, and the detective was told to make an effort to find him.

The night the McCormick boy disappeared his relatives said that he had put on his overcoat at his home at 7 o'clock, preparatory to going to church with two of his sisters, and that he was missed after he had started down to the basement of his home for the purpose of getting his hat. None of the family saw him after he started to get his hat.

Additional light was thrown on this story yesterday when the Rev. Father Mullen, pastor of the Sacred Heart Church in High Bridge, declared that the public had not been told that Willie McCormick had been seen opposite the church half an hour after he had been seen at his home.

"Two boys saw Willie sitting on a fence opposite the church," said the priest. "Willie appeared to be in trouble. He was holding his hands to his head. The boys spoke to him and he jumped down and ran away, saying he was going to his home. They followed him down Martha avenue and one of them, John Horan, remarked 'That's a funny way for Willie to go home. He's going toward Smith's Hotel.' The boys yelled to him, asking him why he was running in that direction. Willie burst out crying and ran on.

### -con't The New York Sun May 12, 1901

"At the point where 169th street and Jerome avenue come together the Horan boy and his companion, a boy known as Burt Thom, parted. Young Horan saw Willie McCormick going toward the woods back of Baird's Hotel, and when he got home he told his mother, Mrs Horan, about it. Capt. Titus of the Detective Bureau investigated this story immediately after the disappearance of the McCormick boy. The Horan boy has repeated it several times since. It was this story that convinced the police that Willie had not been kidnapped, but had probably run away from home. He probably went down along the railroad tracks and was crossing the trestle over Cromwell's Creek when he fell in."

A letter was received at The Sun office last night saying that Willie McCormick had on two occasions been chased by an Italian.

"Willie took up the Italian's hat to tease him, and to get even with the boy the Italian threw Willie into the creek," the letter said. The letter was signed "M. F. Brown."

John T. Hilton, a transit man in the employ of the Dock Department, informed The Sun yesterday he had good reason to doubt that the body of Willie McCormick could have been in the place where it was finally found ever since the boy disappeared. Mr Hilton spent the entire week ending May 4 in that very region, making a map of the shores of Cromwell Creek. He passed over every foot of the crib bulkhead that borders the south shore of the creek, from the Harlem River to 161st street.

He says he saw no sign of a body in the creek. His work being on shore, however, an object in the water might have escaped his observation. But Mr Hilton brings to mind the fact that high tide had set in when the body was found, stuck in the mud, while during the preceding two weeks the water in the creek was much lower.

Mr Hilton further mentioned that Charles W. Thompson, one of the Dock Department's expert hydrographers, led a sounding party that went up and down the creek in a boat several times during the days of April 22-25. Soundings were taken every fifty feet, not only in one place but every five feet from one shore to the other of the creek. Mr Hilton thinks it very unlikely that those men should have failed to find the body, had it been in the creek at the time.

## *The Star Tribune* May 13, 1901

# HOW SEARCH FOR LOST BOY ENDED IN BITTER SORROW

### Discovery of Body of Little Willie McCormick, Lad Who Has Been Missing Six Weeks, Ends Hunt.

NEW YORK, May 13.—The body of Willie McCormick, who disappeared from his home in this city some weeks ago, was found recently in Cromwell creek at One Hundred and Sixty-first street and Railroad avenue. The body was identified by the boy's sister. The parents of the boy said last night that they had abandoned the idea of foul play, and that they believe the boy had been accidentally drowned.

Willie McCormick, who lived at High Bridge, started from his home early on the evening of his disappearance six weeks ago to attend church. On his road he vanished—there is no other way to describe it. The police, his schoolmates, all his friends and relatives, and the friends and relatives of his family scoured the country for miles about his home. Detectives have ransacked all of New York city from Gravesend to the Yonkers line. All the newspapers of the city, and of the entire country for that matter, have been ringing for weeks with the strange story of his disappearance. His picture and his description have been scattered broadcast, and rewards aggregating thousands of dollars have been offered for his return or for news that would lead to the discovery of his whereabouts.

## cond The Star Tribune May 13, 1901

**THE SEARCH FOR THE BOY.**

Detectives have gone here, there, and everywhere trailing clues that seemed promising at first, all of which ended in disappointment. Letters came from all parts of the country describing boys that more or less accurately corresponded with Willie's description. But in every instance the result was the same — only bitter disappointment to the unhappy parents. They at last setttled down to a sort of dull despair in the conviction that the boy had been kidnaped and that the criminals who did the deed had become afraid to restore him, even with the incentive of a large reward.

An extraordinary feature of the McCormick case was the manner of the lad's disappearance. Not a member of the family knew when he left the house or by what door he went out. They merely remembered that after one of his sisters had helped him on with his overcoat he ran down stairs to a basement to get his cap. From that moment not one of them saw him again.

It was about 4 o'clock when he got back from school. He found his father putting up fence posts in the garden back of the house. The father asked Willie to help him with the work, by holding the posts straight while he, the father, stamped in the dirt around them.

The boy was busy at this until 5:30, when he and his father went to the house to tidy themselves for dinner. After Willie had washed his hands and face his mother sent him to the corner grocery, which is rather farther than a short city block away, to get some milk. He went and was gone an unnecessarily long time — 20 minutes or half an hour. About this, however, there was no mystery. Willie McCormick was a 10-year-old boy, and as given to fun as boys usually are at that age. He simply was skylarking with some of his playmates. A neighbor, Mr. Frank Tierney, saw him at this and told him he had better hurry home with the milk or he would have a score to settle with his mother.

## -con't The Star Tribune May 13, 1901

### QUIT HIS SKYLARKING.

Evidently the boy was of the same opinion, for he quit his skylarking and hurried for home. Near his gate he met three more of his acquaintances, Harry Therritt, much older than Willie; Lawrence Tierney, and Adrian McCloud. To these boys Willie said he was going to church as soon as he had had his dinner, and he asked them to go with him. They all declined, for one reason or another. Then Willie went into the house.

This was about 6:30 o'clock. His parents and the other members of the family say that he was not scolded for being so long on his errand. He sat down to the table with the rest of the family and ate such a dinner as a growing boy, who has been to school, been playing, and been helping put in fence posts might be expected to eat. When dinner was over he set about getting ready for church. As he was about this he spoke the last words his mother was destined to hear him speak perhaps forever.

"It will be a bad Easter week for Mrs. Thompson, mamma," he said, "with little Tina lying dead there in the house."

Mrs. Thompson was a neighbor, whose five-year-old child had just died. This had made a strong impression upon Willie McCormick. His mother made some appropriate reply, and the boy then called to his sister Anna and asked her to comb his hair. This Anna did, and Willie was quite minute and explicit in his directions as to how it was to be parted.

*—con't The Star Tribune May 13, 1901*

## GETS READY FOR CHURCH.

These preparations were all made in the basement of the house. Upstairs, in the main entrance hall, the boy's sisters, Gertrude and Sadie, were impatiently waiting for him to go to church with them.

"Come, Willie, hurry up," Gertrude exclaimed, as he at last came running upstairs into the hall. "Hurry up. It's late already, and we must go."

Willie's overcoat was on a rack in the hall, and his sister helped him on with it.

"There," he exclaimed, when he had got the coat on, "I've left my cap downstairs. Go on ahead. I'll run down and get it and catch up with you."

The little fellow started on a run for the back stairs. His sisters did not see him after that moment. They went on out the front door, down the flight of steps in the yard to the street and walked rapidly off in the direction of the church.

There is some uncertainty among the members of the family as to the exact hour that this departure of the two sisters and Willie's hasty run downstairs for his cap took place. Devotions in the church were due to begin at 7:30 and would not last more than half an hour, and as the two girls were only a very little late in arriving at the church, it is probable that the actual time when Willie McCormick disappeared was somewhere very close to 7:20 in the evening. It was the 27th of March, just about one hour after sunset, and consequently dark.

The family knows that Willie went to the dining room from the absence of his cap, but his actual disappearance, the exact point where he vanished from all knowledge of the members of the family was at the head of the stairs leading down to the basement. So far as his father and mother and sisters are concerned, the earth to all intents and purposes swallowed the boy at that place and time.

*—con't The Star Tribune May 13, 1901*

## SEARCH BEGUN AT ONCE.

From that moment began the long agony for that unhappy family, which has known no alleviation to this day. The entire neighborhood was searched. The neighbors were roused out of their beds and joined in the search. At 11:30 o'clock the case was reported to the police, and a general alarm was sent out. The next day began the false "clews" and the false identifications. Willie had been seen in Jerome avenue; he had been seen in half a dozen other places in the neighborhood. A minute search was made that day as far as One Hundred and Eighty-eighth street.

Of alleged clews, which, when probed, proved to be worthless, there were several. And there have been the adventurers trying to make money out of the family's grief. April 2 they received a letter threatening to burn Willie's eyes out unless a certain sum of money was left at a certain designated spot. A few days later a Brooklyn car conductor was sure he had seen and talked with Willie on his car at Coney Island. Then a boy was held at Red Bank until detectives and acquaintances of Willie went and found out that it was not Willie. And so it has gone, letters to this day coming in an unbroken stream and all of them leading to nothing. It was the fixed belief of the police and the fixed belief of Father Mullen for a time that the boy had run away. The police worked on that line alone.

Rewards of $6,000 had been offered for the return of the boy. Of this amount $1,000 was offered by a neighbor of the family, and $5,000 by M. G. McCormick, uncle of the boy. The rewards were offered with the condition "no questions asked."

*—con't The Star Tribune May 13, 1901*

## THE CLUE FROM WASHINGTON.

M. G. McCormick lives in Washington, D. C. Recently, while at the Hoffman house in this city he received a letter from Washington which hinted darkly at knowledge of Willie's whereabouts. Soon after a Washington photographer sent to Mr. McCormick a scrap of paper which he said he had got from a Gypsy. On the paper—which was a bit of white wrapping paper—was written the name "Gertrude," the name of one of Willie McCormick's 11 sisters. He was the only boy in a family of 12 children.

Miss Gertrude McCormick and the rest of the family believed that the scrap of paper was genuine; that in some manner inscrutable to them it came from Willie, for Miss McCormick was sure she recognized the handwriting as her own. There was correspondence with the photographer who sent the bit of paper, but nothing came of it. If anything, the episode only cast a deeper shade of mystery over the entire dark situation.

When Willie McCormick disappeared he had, so far as his parents know, just one cent in money in his possession. His mother had given him that to buy candy with at the corner grocery on his way to church. He never bought the candy.

## *The New York World May 13, 1901*

# BOYS WEEP FOR DEAD COMPANION

## Schoolmates' Tears and Flowers for Willie McCormick.

The last chapter of the Highbridge tragedy ended this morning when the body of Willie McCormick was placed in the grave at St. Raymond's Cemetery, Throgg's Neck. The white casket was borne by ten of the playmates of the boy whose disappearance six weeks ago aroused the whole country, and the whole population of Highbridge crowded about the house and church to give evidence of their sympathy.

The flag which usually floats over Public School No. 91 was not flying to-day, and the 600 pupils were dismissed by Principal McGuire. They stood about the house and in front of the church, silent and awe-struck by the ceremony which marked the end in the brief history of their little comrade.

The pall-bearers were Lanny Tierney, Jimmy Lyons, Willie Lyons, Adrian McCloud, Owney Jones, Harry Van Wagoner, Tony Murray, Joe Denny, Tobey Fitzpatrick and Earl Fisterious. Six students from Manhattan College, where Willie was a favorite, walked beside the hearse.

The mother was more composed this morning and no longer denied that the body was that of her son, but the father cannot forget his great loss in his only son. "He is the last of the McCormicks," the old gentleman repeats softly.

Rev. Father John A. Mullin conducted low mass at the Church of the Sacred Heart, in Marcher avenue, at 10 o'clock, and ten carriages followed the body to the cemetery. The house and church were both filled to overflowing. The plate on the casket bore this inscription:

"Willie J. McCormick, died March 27, 1901, aged 10 years and 2 months."

New York Times May 14, 1901

## FUNERAL OF WILLIE McCORMICK

### Large Crowds Followed the Cortege to the Church—Father Mullin's Eulogy.

The body of Willie McCormick was buried yesterday morning. Crowds of people, friends and relatives of the family, were at the house early and many other gathered outside.

As early as 8 o'clock callers began coming to the McCormick home, at Ogden Avenue and One Hundred and Sixty-fifth Street. The body of the boy lay in a copper sealed casket inside a white plush casket. On the outer casket was a silver plate bearing the inscription:

> WILLIE J. McCORMICK,
> Aged 10 Years and 2 Months.
> Died March 27, 1901.

March 27 was the day on which Willie disappeared.

The casket was almost entirely covered with flowers, and the rear of the room was filled with bouquets, wreaths, crosses, and other emblems. A large pillow, with "Our Darling Boy," was at the foot of the casket.

*—Cont' New York Times May 14, 1901*

Ten playmates and schoolmates of Willie acted as honorary pall bearers. They were Lancelot Tierney, James and William Lyons, Andrew McLeod, Tobias Fitzpatrick, Joseph Denny, Anthony Murray, Harry Van Wagener, Owen Jones, and Carl Cistorius. Each of them had around the right sleeve a white ribbon with a white rosette. The regular pall bearers were six young men from Manhattan College. Willie often used to watch the college boys play ball, and he had become quite a favorite. The pall bearers were Edward F. Roche, G. W. Potter, J. F. Sullivan, Thomas D. McCarthy, James Plunkitt, and Thomas J. Kearns.

In the church were 160 schoolmates of the dead boy, all from Public School No. 91, on Ogden Avenue. Their principal, John McGuire, was present in charge of them. The mass was celebrated by Father Mullin, who offered the large reward for the recovery of the boy. He was assisted by Father Burke of St. Philip's, in Bedford Park; Father Slattery of St. Catherine of Geona, and Father Mahoney of St. Charles Borromeo's. The acolytes were schoolmates of the boy.

In the course of his eulogy of the dead boy Father Mullin said:

"This boy may be detained a little time for his childish sins, but I firmly believe he will be in heaven very soon. I wish I were as sure of getting to heaven as he, even if I had to be detained a thousand years. All Christian mothers' prayers will go out to this poor mother in her affliction in the loss of her boy. Do not ask me if the boy strayed away. Do not ask me if he ran away. Do not ask me if he was kidnapped. Do not ask me if he was murdered. I do not know."

The body of the boy was blessed by Father Mullin, and the benediction was pronounced, closing the service. The interment took place in St. Raymond's Cemetery, in Westchester.

## *New York Times* May 13, 1901

## Funeral of the Drowned Boy Will Be Held This Morning.

### Suicide Theory Is Scouted by Relatives —Death by Accident Also Denied —Police Criticised.

The body of Willie McCormick will be buried this morning. The services will be conducted in St. Mary's Church, in Nelson Avenue, High Bridge, by the Rev. Father Mullin, who will say a low mass and use the ordinary burial service.

Father Mullin agreed with Mr. McCormick that a high mass would take too much time, and on account of the feeble condition of Mrs. McCormick, who insists on attending the service, it was accordingly agreed to shorten the ordeal as much as possible.

Hundreds of people went to the McCormick house yesterday. They began to call in the early morning and the neighbors and intimate friends who sat up throughout the night were relieved when daylight came. People from far-distant points of Brooklyn, Queens, Manhattan, and Richmond Boroughs were present, and some from New Jersey called to offer their condolences. The double parlors were filled with floral tributes. Some of the handsomest pieces came from total strangers.

The neighbors in High Bridge absolutely decline to accept the police theory that the boy's death was the result of drowning by accident. Criticism of what they term the "carelessness of the police" were numerous, and some were bitter in the extreme. Frank Tierney, a next door neighbor of the McCormick family, said the latest theory of suicide by the boy was the most cruel blow the family had suffered.

## *The Brooklyn Daily Eagle May 13, 1901*

### WILLIE MC CORMICK BURIED.

#### Service Held This Morning in the Church of the Sacred Heart.

The funeral of Willie McCormick, whose body after more than a month's search for him was found in Cromwell Creek, last Saturday, took place this morning from the boy's home, One Hundred and Sixty-first street and Ogden avenue.

The pall bearers were six young men from Manhattan College with whose students young McCormick was a general favorite, but ten of the former playmates and school friends of the boy were selected as honorary pall bearers. At 10 o'clock the body was moved to the Church of the Sacred Heart, where mass was celebrated by Father Mullin, who offered a large reward for the recovery of the boy. He was assisted by Father Burke of St. Philip's in Bedford Park, Father Slattery of St. Catharile of Genoa's, Father Mahoney of St. Charles Borromeo's churches. The church was crowded, nearly all the boy's school mates being present.

### Weekly Cannon Register May 16, 1901

### THREATENED A WHIPPING.

#### Then Willie McCormick Ran Away From Home and Was Drowned.

New York, May 11—Rev. Father Mullen said today that Willie McCormick, long believed to have been kidnapped, and who was found drowned yesterday, ran away from home in fear of a beating. The boy had received a note from his teacher threatening to whip him. This note was sent on the day before the boy disappeared.

## Final Resting Place

The McCormick Family left the Highbridge neighborhood in the late 1920s. They moved to Springfield, Massachusetts. The family had the body of Little Willie disinterred from Saint Raymond's Cemetery in the Bronx and re-buried at St. Michael's Cemetery in Springfield.

William McCormick
BIRTH     1891
DEATH     1901 (aged 9–10)
BURIAL
Saint Michael's Cemetery
Springfield, Hampden County, Massachusetts, USA
PLOT     St Benedicts B/C

## Coroner's Report

Race:     White
Marital status:     Single
Age:     10
Birth Date:     Abt. 1891
Birth Place:     City
Residence Street Address:     Ogden Ave, High Bridge
Death Date:     May 1901
Death Street Address:     Corneille Park
Death Place:     New York City, Bronx, New York, USA
Cause of Death:     Submersion
Burial Date:     13 May 1901
Burial Place:     St. Raymond's
Occupation:     School Boy
Father's Birth Place:     Ireland
Mother's Birth Place:     Ireland

# Cromwell's Creek

This is part of Cromwell's Creek, near the area where Willie's body was found.

The section of the Creek where Willie's body was discovered was 300 feet from where it emptied into the Harlem River. The brackish water where the fresh waters of Cromwell's Creek emptied into the river was a favorite fishing and crabbing spot for local fishermen.

There were so many crabs and eels in this area that the small island in the Harlem River at the mouth of the creek was named Crab Island.

For those who may not be familiar with the Harlem River. It's really not a river. It's a branch of an estuary that eventually connects to the Atlantic Ocean.

The Harlem River forms a part of the Hudson estuary system, serving as a narrow strait that divides the island of Manhattan from the Bronx. The tides of the Hudson Estuary of which the Harlem River is part, are affected by the tides of the Atlantic ocean. The confluence of the freshwater from Cromwells Creek intermingling with the saltwater tide feeding the Hudson River estuary created the perfect conditions for crabs, eels, and other brackish water creatures to proliferate.

The area where Little Willie's body was found had been thoroughly searched by the police and volunteers.

For several weeks before the finding of the body, a team of municipal surveyors had been plotting the creek and the lands adjacent to the swampy real estate.

Their statements indicated, that if a body had been in the water when they were surveying, they would have noticed.

The residents of the Highbridge neighborhood, the men and boys who trapped crabs in the brackish waters for a living disagreed with the police who claimed that the body had been in the water for more than six weeks. And the easy identification by Willie's sister indicated that all of his features were still easily recognized.

As for the autopsy, coroners at that time were usually politically appointed positions. Most coroners in 1900 were not even physicians. However, because of the notoriety of Willie's death, a physician, Doctor Riegelman, did assist in the original autopsy. After the original autopsy, there was an outcry from Willie's family, friends, neighbors, and others who did not believe the boy was in the water or at the location where the body was found for more than six weeks.

The body underwent a second autopsy. The results of the second autopsy were never released to the public.

# Epilogue

The cause of death was never accepted by the McCormick family, the public, or anyone who knew him.

As you know by reading the newspaper articles from 1901, Willie McCormick was afraid of the dark and afraid of water. So finding his body in the brackish waters of Cromwell's Creek made no sense whatsoever to anyone in the Bronx neighborhood where Willie lived.

So why was the case of the missing boy closed so quickly after finding the remains of the child? Well, there are a plethora of reasons as to why the Police wanted to bury the case along with Willie McCormick.

From the start, any armchair sleuth who has any forensic knowledge at all about the correct manner to proceed in a missing child case knows, without a doubt, that the entire investigation was flawed from day one.

My goodness, for a Captain of the Police to let the press take over and sensationalize every single clue and tip related to the investigation is madness. Pure and simple madness.

One fact, that the newspapers barely touched upon was the phenomenal amount of graft that existed at the time.

New York City in 1900 was a gold mine for corrupt cops. And for a Police Captain to be sent to the Bronx meant you had stepped on the wrong toes and were most likely being put out to pasture by higher-ranking officials at Police Headquarters in Manhattan.

Midtown and lower Manhattan were where a Police Captain, and those under him, the trusted ones who followed his orders, could and did make a fortune.

The illegal gambling joints, the houses of ill-repute, the loan sharks, the protection racket, the corrupt judges and politicians were the fertile grounds where a smart cop could put away enough money in less than a year to retire for life. However, greed being what it is, few cops fulfilled their dream of early retirement.

# Father Mullin

Who was Father Mullin and why was he so quick to offer a reward of $10,000 for the safe return of Willie McCormack?

In today's value, $10,000 in 1901 currency would be more than $350,000.

So, tell me, where would this Bronx Parish Priest get the money to pay the ransom Father Mullin offered of $10,000? There are no records as to where the money would have come from.

And it should be noted that upon the death of Father Mullin in 1907, there were legal issues about his real estate holdings in the Bronx.

From 1875 when church officials sent him to the Highbridge neighborhood to start a Mission, Father Mullin purchased properties with church funds that were recorded as personal property in his name. Upon his passing, the New York Arch-Diocese sought and received relief through court proceedings.

The fact that he offered a reward would have, in today's world of criminal investigative procedures, made Father James Mullin a person of interest. Yet despite the number of conflicting public statements and suppositions Father Mullins made about Little Willie, he was never vetted by the police or the press.

When it comes to Father Mullin, the man seems to leave a Red Herring everywhere he can. The sheer number of statements to the press seems to me, to have been intended to mislead and distract the police from their investigation.

Let us not forget, the power a Catholic Priest wielded over his parishioners in the early 1900s. Nor should we dismiss the circumstances that surrounded the McCormick family at the time Willie vanished. Mr. McCormick was in New York

City's infamous Ludlow Street Jail for more than two years preceding the disappearance of his son.

During this period when the father was absent from the home, little Willie was likely the most spoiled kid in the neighborhood. Can you imagine being the only male child in a family with 11 sisters, and being younger than 9 of them?

We do know from several newspaper reports, that Willie developed some poor behavioral habits while his father was incarcerated.

So where does the Priest fit in? Father Mullin's off-the-cuff comments to the press indicate that he knew Little Willie fairly well. We also know, from newspaper reports, that the ten-year-old had a lot on his mind the evening he left his home to catch up with his sisters on their way to church.

Willie knew that he was in trouble at school. We know from several newspaper articles that Willie was part of a group of boys who were harassing the immigrant workers of a local building contractor. Mr. Jones, the owner of the construction company had spoken with Willie's parents about his misdeeds. And when this chronic misbehavior continued, Mr. Jones went to Willie's school, PS 91, and spoke with the Principal, Mr. McGuire.

A note had been sent home from his teacher the day Willie vanished about a disciplinary action waiting for Willie.

We also know there were reports of at least 2 separate incidents about Willie being accosted by a stranger in the neighborhood who wanted the little boy to come with him.

Plus, the newspapers reported that two younger men had chased Willie home from school a few days earlier.

So, we have one heck of a scared little boy who suddenly found himself in a world of the proverbial self-created bucket of trouble.

What options at this point does a 10-year-old have? Did he think the only person who could help him was the Priest?

The cultural mindset of most Irish-Catholic families, in America at that time, placed all Priests on a very high pedestal. The local parish Priests were prime influencers of the political and social views of his "flock", the men, women, and children who sat in the pews every Sunday morning and attentively listened to every word he had composed and spoke from the pulpit.

I often wonder, about the interactions of Father Mullin with Little Willie and the McCormack Family while Mr. McCormick sat in jail for more than 2 years.

*New York Times June 3, 1907*

**PUBLIC NOTICES.**

Pursuant to statutory requirement, notice is hereby given that an act, Senate 1,481, Int. No. 199, has been passed by both branches of the Legislature, entitled

AN ACT
TO AUTHORIZE THE COMMISSIONERS OF THE SINKING FUND OF THE CITY OF NEW YORK, IN BEHALF OF SAID CITY, TO COMPROMISE, SETTLE, CANCEL, ANNUL, AND DISCHARGE CERTAIN TAXES AND ASSESSMENTS AND INTEREST THEREON LEVIED UPON THE PROPERTY THE LEGAL TITLE TO WHICH IS IN THE NAME OF JAMES A. MULLIN, PASTOR OF THE CHURCH OF THE SACRED HEART, IN SAID CITY, SITUATED IN THE TWENTY-THIRD WARD OF THE CITY OF NEW YORK, BOROUGH OF THE BRONX.

Further notice is hereby given that a Public Hearing upon such bill will be held at the Mayor's office, in the City Hall, in the City of New York, on Wednesday, June 5th, 1907, at 10:30 o'clock A. M.

Dated City Hall, New York, June 1st, 1907.

GEORGE B. McCLELLAN,
Mayor.

This bill will be the second heard at that time.

**Father James A. Mullin**

*The press and official government records used several spellings of the name Mullin when referring to Father Mullin. Besides Mullin, they used Mullins, Mullen, Mullens, and possibly a few more. While trying to trace the family roots of this man, because of the various spellings used by the Government, the Church, and the Priest, plus other roadblocks I came across, I was unable to verify his birthplace which he claims was in Ireland. I was also unable to verify the country or year of his Ordination.

The 1870 Federal Census shows Father James A. Mullin in Orange County New York. Over the years, he reported 4 different birth years to the Federal Government. It is also interesting to note; that when answering the questionnaire for the census taker, he reported that he was unable to read or write. I find that very unusual for a priest. However, the accuracy of the census is often the cause of discrepancies.

*In 1870 Orange County was, and still is, part of the Archdiocese of New York.*

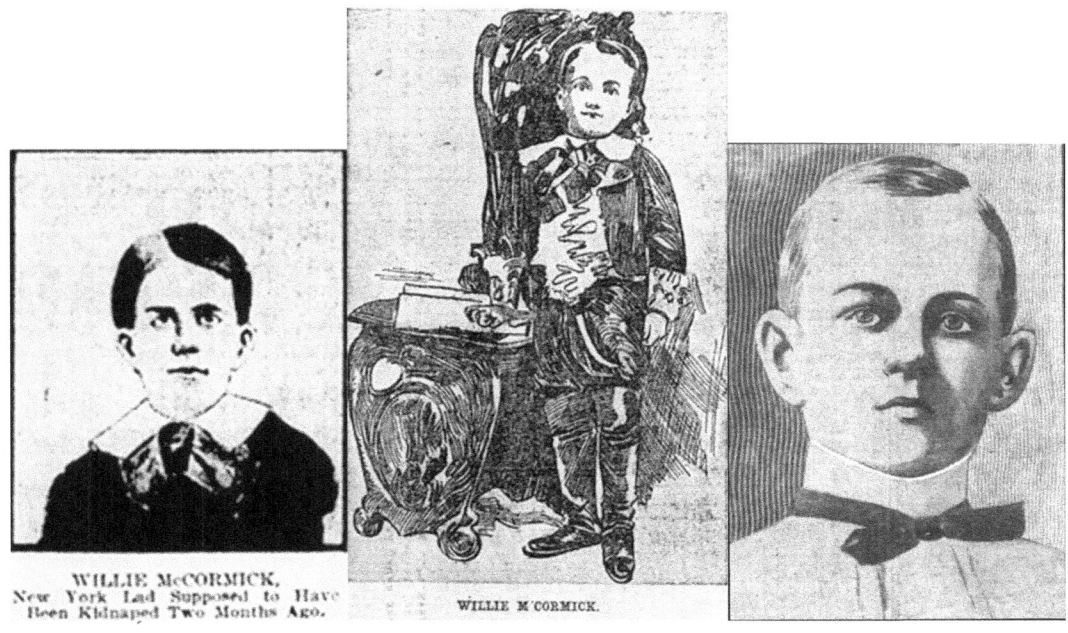

**Various Photos & Drawings of Willie McCormick Circulated by Newspapers across the USA.**

Looking at these different images, I can see why so many people with good intentions reported seeing a boy they thought might be Willie McCormick.

What Really Happened  Pat Fogarty

| Name | Relation | | | Birth | Age | | | | Birthplace | Father | Mother | | | Occupation |
|---|---|---|---|---|---|---|---|---|---|---|---|---|---|---|
| McCormick W | Head | W | M | Jan 1841 | 59 | m | 26 | | Ireland | Ireland | Ireland | 1860 | 40 Na | |
| — Margaret | Wife | W | F | June 1852 | 48 | m | 26 | 12/12 | Ireland | Ireland | Ireland | 1863 | 37 | |
| — Rose | Daughter | W | F | June 1868 | 31 | S | | | New Hampshire | Ireland | Ireland | | | Bookkeeper - Grocery |
| — Marcella | Daughter | W | F | Aug 1876 | 24 | S | | | New Hampshire | Ireland | Ireland | | | Teacher School |
| — Margaret | Daughter | W | F | Jan 1878 | 22 | S | | | New Hampshire | Ireland | Ireland | | | Teacher School |
| — Anna | Daughter | W | F | Jan 1880 | 20 | S | | | New Jersey | Ireland | Ireland | | | Typewriter |
| — Susan | Daughter | W | F | Aug 1882 | 18 | S | | | New Jersey | Ireland | Ireland | | | Typewriter |
| — Carmelita | Daughter | W | F | July 1884 | 15 | S | | | New Jersey | Ireland | Ireland | | | At School |
| — Sarah | Daughter | W | F | Dec 1886 | 13 | S | | | New York | Ireland | Ireland | | | At School |
| — Gertrude | Daughter | W | F | Oct 1888 | 12 | S | | | New York | Ireland | Ireland | | | At School |
| — William | Son | W | M | Feb 1891 | 9 | S | | | New York | Ireland | Ireland | | | |
| — Beatrice | Daughter | W | F | Apr 1893 | 7 | S | | | New York | Ireland | Ireland | | | |
| — Isabell | Daughter | W | F | Jan 1895 | 5 | S | | | New York | Ireland | Ireland | | | |

## 1900 Federal Census Bronx New York

Today a social worker, psychologist, or just about anyone with a decent knowledge of childhood development might come up with the idea; that having eleven sisters, a doting mother, and no father at home for two years might make a big difference in the behavioral development of a young boy.

I also find it difficult to understand why his parents did not take action when Mr. Jones went to them about Willie's wrongdoings.

I often wonder if Mr. Jones spoke with just the mother and not both parents? And if he had just spoken with Mrs. McCormick; did she tell her husband of their son's follies?

Another part of the investigation that I have trouble with is the fact that the wealthy investors Mr. McCormick defrauded are barely mentioned. Who were they? Supposedly it was a very large amount of money. And when the Courts adjudicated the fraud case against Mr. McCormick; there were no orders or provisions made by the Judge about any monies being repaid.

We also know with the newspapers and their reporters so involved in running down clues and coming up with all sorts of theories, why were the men who Mr. McCormick defrauded out of large sums of money not mentioned more often by the press?

We now know the McCormick family, who owned one of the largest and finest homes in the Highbridge neighborhood, the family fared well financially while Mr. McCormick served his 2 years sentence in New York's infamous Ludlow Street Jail;

a jail where it was common knowledge that anyone with money could get anything they wanted while doing their time.

I also find it perplexing that Mrs. McCormick fainted when she heard her son had not met up with his sisters at the church on the night he went missing.

The initial assumption she expressed when she heard the news of her son's disappearance pertained to kidnappers harming her child because of money owed to her husband's creditors.

It is my personal belief; that Mrs. McCormack, who lived without any money worries while her husband spent 2 years in jail, likely knew more about the money her husband had fleeced from his creditors.

The whole scheme for which Mr. McCormick spent 2 years in jail was a classic case of 2 recently purchased warehouses that he claimed were filled with a valuable shipment of flowers from South America. McCormick had heavily insured the contents of the two warehouses, but not the actual warehouses. The money he used to purchase the two large warehouses near the NYC docks came from a recently formed real-estate partnership with several wealthy investors.

Unfortunately, a big fire broke out and spread to both warehouses a few days after the insurance policy was finalized. The insurance company paid for the lost contents in the warehouses with a big check to Mr. McCormick.

However, as the structures were not part of the policy, all the wealthy investors in the real-estate partnership were out of luck. And because the investors were not partners in Mr. McCormick's Wholesale Flower business, they were not entitled to any of the money paid to Mr. McCormick for his insured product, the valuable shipment of flowers.

Yet, because of several legal irregularities in the real-estate partnership, Mr. Mc Cormick was sentenced to serve 2 years in the Ludlow Street Jail for a series of low-level white-collar crimes. I feel it is quite understandable that his creditors were upset and angry that they never got a monetary return on their investment.

# Detective Joseph Petrosino

Detective Joseph Petrosino was born in Italy. He emigrated with his parents to New York City. As a young man, Joseph joined the NYPD and became a pioneer in the fight against organized crime. He especially went after those criminals who preyed on the newly arriving Italian immigrants who came to America seeking a better life. Because of his ability to interrogate Italian criminals in their native tongue, he became the head of "The Italian Squad" which investigated all crimes tied to Italian criminals.

*April 20, 1901*

> Detectives Petrosini and Doran of Police Headquarters were in High Bridge yesterday working on the case, and the former spent his time among the Italian laborers, one of whom is believed by Mrs. McCormick to be responsible for the disappearance of her boy with others had been in the habit of teasing the men. Petrosini reported, however, that he could find none who had cherished any special animosity to the boy, and, in fact, those who remembered him agreed that he had been less aggressive than any of the others.

    Detective Joe Petrosino (sic Peetrosini) was the Detective who questioned some of the workers Willie McCormick and his friends had harassed.

    The men Petrosino questioned told the Detective that Little Willie was not as bad as the other kids who did most of the harassment. However, the older man who had threatened Willie was nowhere to be found when the Detective questioned the rest of the crew.

After speaking with the Italian workers in their own language, Petrosino interviewed Mr. Jones about the older worker who was not with the other workers when he spoke with them. Mr. Jones, the owner of the construction company told the Detective that he did not know the name of the individual the Detective wanted to speak with. Mr. Jones said he did not keep any records of the men who worked for him.

Here's another confusing irregularity in a proper police investigation of a missing child.

Everyone knew the family blamed one of the Italian masons who was harassed by Willie and his friends. The family believed the man had something to do with the disappearance of their son. The Parents reported an incident to the police where it was known that the man had chased Willie.

So, tell me why it took more than three weeks to send an Italian-speaking detective to question the workers?

## *The Delaware Morning News May 13, 1901*

"I still believe my boy was murdered," said Mr. McCormick, "and the fact that the autopsy shows that death was due to drowning does not do away with the belief held by me and my friends that Willie was murdered. I have received information to the effect that on several occasions my boy was chased by an Italian whom he had teased. This Italian was a laborer and I asked the police to find him, but they tell me that the Italian had nothing whatever to do with the case. My poor boy was certainly murdered, for he never could have fallen into that creek accidentally."

Detective Petrosini, the Italian sleuth of the Central Office, was detailed on the case yesterday for the purpose of running down this story. He reported to Captain Titus last night that he could get no verification of the story. The Italian who was said to have figured in the case had left High Bridge, and the detective was told to make an effort to find him.

And, who told Detective Petrosino to make no effort to find the missing worker? Was it CaptainTitus or was it the Detective's Commander at Police headquarters? Corruption in the NYPD in 1901 was a big problem. Without too much effort you will find many books and stories about the influence of *The Black Hand* or maybe better known by the name *The Mafia*, and how these criminal organizations bribed Politicians, Judges, and Police Commanders.

After reading all these old newspaper articles, I can understand the reason why so many people in 1901 believed the New York Police Department bungled the disappearance of Little Willie McCormick from day one. The facts reported by the press of 1901 tell a story of total incompetence.

But to have the authorities close the case without speaking with the most obvious person of interest, the old Italian man who threatened and chased Willie, is extremely suspicious. However, because the entire country knew just how badly the case was handled, it is understandable that the Big Brass at Police Headquarters wanted to wash their proverbial hands of an unsolved crime and get it out of the newspapers as fast as possible.

The Family, the neighbors, the men and women who knew the neighborhood and who also knew Little Willie, the policemen who patrolled the entire Highbridge community on foot and horseback, and the fishermen who earned a living by trapping blue crabs and catching eels in the brackish waters of Cromwell creek; all of them as a collective group, they could not believe that Little Willie McCormick went on his own accord to Cromwell's Creek on the night of March 27, 1901. Nor could they believe the boy accidentally drowned or far worse, as some unscrupulous newspapers wrote, that he may have committed suicide.

First and foremost, if Willie had been in the water for more than six weeks, neither his sister nor anyone else would have been able to recognize the boy, especially with the ease 12-year-old Gertrude McCormick identified her little brother.

As for the coroner's physician's statement, that the boy had drowned by falling into the water, and the physician saying; he did not know if Willie was conscious or unconscious when he fell into the creek? Well to me, it seems like someone was doing more speculation than scientific studying.

Also, every fisherman who made a living fishing and crabbing in the brackish tidal waters of Cromwell Creek knew if the boy had been in the creek since he disappeared, the crabs, eels, and other varmin in and around the swampy waters would have made Willie's corpse unrecognizable to the extreme extent. Some even said all the flesh would have been eaten away if the body had been in the water for that length of time.

And as for the physician saying there were no marks of violence on the boy's features except for a small cut on his cheek, well, once again, that contradicts common sense. It was a relatively warm spring, the creek was more like a swamp that a running creek. It rarely froze, even in the dead of winter. The water was mostly salty for about four hundred yards inland. Willies body was found less than 50 yards inland. No raging waters were coming from or going to the Harlem River, which as previously mentioned was part of the Hudson Estuary and not a true river. The Harlem river rises and falls with the tides of the Atlantic Ocean which by the time the tides reach the Bronx, are very gentle and subtle.

And what about the stench of a dead body and the above-ground wildlife in the area. Aquatic and scavenger birds made their homes in the trees and weeds of the swampy creek. The area where the body was found was not secluded. The area was easily viewed from a nearby bridge that traversed a portion of the creek.

Again, with so many unanswered questions from the coroner and the investigators—the family, the neighbors, and most folks familiar with the incident, never accepted the theory that it was an accident.

## Oscar Wilgerodt

Name: Oscar E F Willgerodt
Gender: Male
Marriage Date: 8 Oct 1885
Marriage Place: Manhattan, New York, USA
Certificate Number: 51180

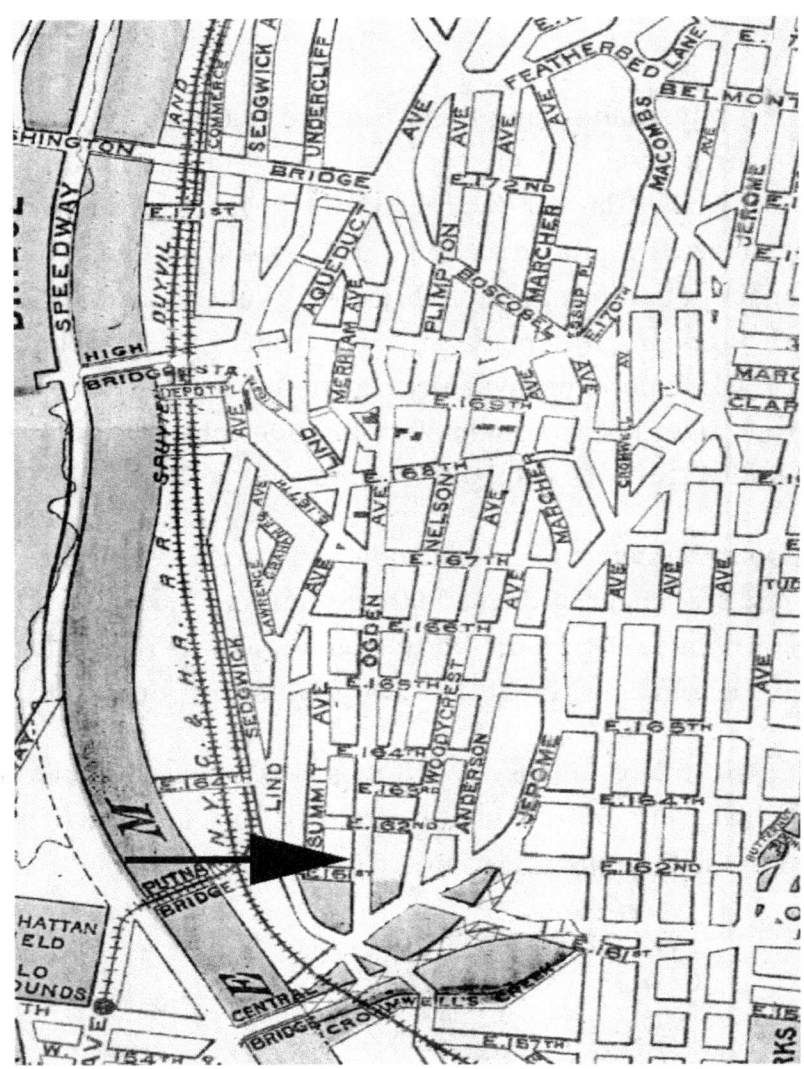

**The tip of the arrow shows the location of the Willgerodt Home**

*The Buffalo Inquirer April 3, 1901, mentions Oscar Wilgerodt*

## BOY MAY HAVE BECOME A JOCKEY

### Latest Theory Regarding the Mysterious Disappearance of Willie McCormick.

[SPECIAL TELEGRAM TO THE ENQUIRER.]

New York, April 3.—William McCormick, the 10-year-old boy who disappeared last Wednesday, is still missing. The police today have a new theory. It is thought the lad ran away to become a jockey.

The theory is based on the story of a trolley car conductor of Brooklyn that he carried to the race track a boy resembling young McCormick.

Oscar Wilgerodt, a wealthy neighbor of the McCormick family, has offered $1,000 for the safe return of the boy. The pleadings of Wilgerodt's son, a playmate of the missing boy, prompted the generous offer.

Looking back, it seems a bit odd that Oscar Willgerodt would make such a generous offer so quickly. A thousand dollars in 1901 was equivalent to $35,000 to $40,000 in today's value.

And, although Mr. Willgerodt claimed, in one of his statements to the press, that the reason he offered the reward was that his son, Oscar junior, was crying and upset with the disappearance of his friend.

As we can see from the birth records, Oscar Jr. was 2 years younger than Willie and although Oscar attended the same primary school as little Willie, there is nothing that indicates the two boys were friends.

Willie walked to school every day with some of the older boys in the neighborhood. Oscar junior was driven to and from school by horse and buggy which was driven by Mr. Willgerodt's coachman.

## Willgerodt Marrige Record

*Multiple spellings of non-Anglo-Saxon surnames were common during the late 19th and early 20th centuries.

| | |
|---|---|
| Name: | Oscar Rich. Lud. Willgocodt |
| Gender: | Male |
| Race: | White |
| Birth Date: | 24 Apr 1893 |
| Birth Place: | Manhattan, New York City, New York, New York, USA |
| Residence Address: | ChriStreetopher Street 25 |
| Certificate Number: | 21520 |
| Father: | Oscar Willgocodt |
| Mother: | Bertha Willgocodt |
| Mother Maiden Name: | Schilling |

*1900 Census * end of page 1: continued on next full census page*

## 1915 NY Census

Oscar Wilgerodt was a shrewd businessman. Oscar was in the coat business. He owned several coat stores at different times in lower Manhattan. Sometimes he ran these coat stores as the sole owner and sometimes he worked with a partner.

Fortunately, most real estate transactions at the turn of the 19th to 20th century in NYC were recorded in newspapers. Oscar's footprints in the real estate and property mortgage markets were very well recorded.

The man, for a time, was a successful merchant. However, there were times when he struggled and took out mortgages to help finance his endeavors. His home in 1901 on Ogden Avenue was one of the finer homes in the area. It was a large home with ample room for a cook, housekeeper, gardener, and coachman. Which, according to the full 1900 Willgerodt Federal Census, Oscar employed these four servants as members of his household; meaning they also resided at the home on Ogden Avenue.

It's also very interesting that Oscar Willgerodt put his home up for sale and sold it shortly after the discovery of Little Willie's body.

Coincident? You decide. Oscar Willgerodt's motive for moving?

He may have been feeling a bit of a financial pinch.

When Mr. Wilgerodt sold their Ogden Avenue home, the family moved into a large 7-room apartment in the University Heights section of the Bronx. In the opinion of many; this was not exactly a move up in the social standings of the Willgerodt family.

But, Oscar and his family were still living well.

The 1915 New York State Census shows, that besides his wife and children, he still employed at least one live-in servant.

As time moved on, the coat business in NYC did not fare as well as Mr. Wilgerodt had expected. By 1920 Oscar and his now failing coat stores had moved out of New York City. The family moved to Springfield, Massachusetts, and opened a coat store.

The coat store in Springfield did not do well. Hugo Willgerodt, Mr. Wilgerodt's second son and younger brother of Oscar junior, was working for his father as a "Floor Walker" at the Springfield store. With the store failing, Oscar and his son Hugo came up with, what they thought was the perfect plan.

The father and son team purchased an inflated amount of fire insurance for their Springfield store which the father had named, *Will & Co.*

Well, as fate would have it, things did not work out so well for Oscar Willlgerodt and his son Hugo.

The Springfield Fire Department, aided by a private detective agency hired by the Hartford Insurance company did a thorough investigation as to the cause of the fire.

In December of 1920 Oscar and Hugo were arrested on various counts of fraud and arson.

The pair were convicted in February of 1921 and Hugo was sent off to prison. Oscar, who by then, was in very poor health received probation and was permitted to return to New York City where he died in August of 1923.

## The Buffalo Inquirer February 7, 1921

### COURT SUSPENDS FOR DAY ON ACCOUNT OF STORK

*(Special Telegram to The Enquirer.)*

Worcester, Mass., Feb. 5.—The stork caused a suspension of the trial in the superior criminal court of Oscar Willgerodt and his son, Hugo Willgerodt, who are under indictment on a charge of setting fire to the Will & Co. store in the State Mutual building

When the case was about to be resumed, word was received by Judge Webster Thayer that District Attorney Edward T. Esty's wife had been taken to Memorial hospital during the night and he had gone with her.

Judge Thayer called off the hearing until afternoon and then word was received that the stork had brought a daughter to District Attorney and Mrs. Estey, so the trial was suspended for a day.

**The Ogden Avenue home of the Willgerodt Family**

The home on Ogden Avenue stood on the same spot until a few years ago when it was demolished to make room for a small apartment building.

## New York Times August 14, 1901

### IN THE REAL ESTATE FIELD

**West Forty-fifth Street Houses Change Hands—Other Dealings by Brokers and at Auction.**

John Hindly has sold, through Greene & Taylor, the two three-story dwellings 41 and 43 West Forty-fifth Street, each 12.6 by 100.5.

George A. Hampton & Brother have sold for Rosa Doctor to S. Cahnmann the five-story three-family flat 1,804 Amsterdam Avenue, 25 by 100.

Janpole & Werner are the buyers of the plot, 50 by 100, on the north side of One Hundred and Twenty-ninth Street, 100 feet east of Eighth Avenue, sold recently through McVickar & Co.

D. Sylvan Crakow has sold for Michael Scanlon to Elias Stone, for $20,000, the five-story single flat 112 East Tenth Street, 18 by 65.

D. Kempner & Son have sold for Antonio Minaldi to Herman Weaver, for about $45,000, the five-story building 605 Eighth Avenue, 25 by 80.

H. Weisstock has sold for H. P. Ansorge, for $67,500, the two five-story double flats 141 and 143 West One Hundred and Thirteenth Street, 50 by 100.11; also, for Oscar Willgerodt, for $22,500, a dwelling on One Hundred and Sixty-first Street, near Ogden Avenue, 45 by 100.

Mr. Wilgerodt sold his Ogden Avenue home in August 1901 for the sum of $22,500; which according to economists would have a cash value of nearly $800,000 today.

## *The New York Herald Statesmen April 26, 1934*

# Suspect Denies Link To Band Of Gem Thieves

## Former Convict Fights Efforts to Involve Him in Society Robbery Series

By United Press

NEW YORK, April 26. — Hugo Willgerodt, former convict, confessed today to participating in jewel robberies totalling $41,500 but fought all efforts to link him with the band credited with stealing more than $1,000,000 in gems from prominent women, police announced after an all-night questioning.

The former floor walker, arrested in Englewood, N. J., admitted, police said, that he helped James Brady and Arthur Rose, now serving prison sentences for the crimes, rob Mrs. Marjorie Ardell of $17,500 in jewelry and Miss Gertrude Williams, former Follies girl, who later committed suicide, of $24,000 in gems.

### Robberies Netted Him $400

"We took flower pots to Mrs. Ardell's apartment to force our way in under the guise of delivery men," police quoted Willgerodt as saying. "We got in and found Mrs. Ardell in bed. Rose was waiting outside in the car."

"Get up," the bandits ordered.

"I can't," Willgerodt said she pleaded, "because I have only a thin robe on."

*-cont.*

### Refuse Mink Coat

Mrs. Ardell asked the men to leave while she dressed but they refused. Finally Willgerodt found a heavy robe in a bureau drawer and threw it to her. A search of the apartment produced only a $15,000 bracelet and a few other trinkets.

"Is this all you got?" the thieves demanded. "We know you got more."

"You might take my mink coat," said the terrified woman. The bandits laughed.

"What are we going to do with a mink coat."

The Williams robbery was executed in similar fashion Willgerodt said, according to police, and the bandit trio celebrated by getting drunk. The prisoner said he had been "lying low" for the past three years supported by his mother and his common-law wife.

The names of persons Willgerodt is accused of robbing resemble a social register. The trail that Lieutenant Michael McNamara and Sergeant Thomas Fitzgerald followed before they captured him took them from a lonely graveyard to a birth certificate, through voluminous records of utility companies and along the dim path of deserted love.

McNamara and Fitzgerald were assigned to the case after the Lucrezia Bori robbery. They learned that Willgerodt formerly had been a floorwalker and purportedly gained information for thefts by coming into contact with wealthy patrons.

*-cont.*

> Learning that his father was buried in Woodlawn Cemetery, they kept a vigil at the grave for weeks vainly hoping he might visit it.
>
> Diligent search revealed that Willgerodt was married and that his wife and four children lived in Manhattan. But after they found his wife they learned he had deserted her four years ago.
>
> **Girl's Refuses Aid**
>
> Learning that he was living with a Barbara Jaffe in New Jersey and that they had one child, the detectives rummaged through years of birth certificates and found the one they were seeking. Posing as relief agents, they went to Miss Jaffe's father but he would give no information.
>
> They searched through all the records of New York utilities companies looking for a Barbara Jaffe. Finding none, they went through the files of New Jersey companies. There they uncovered the name and address they sought.
>
> Enlisting the aid of a laundry wagon driver, the detectives went to the home and watched while he went to the door. Inside they saw the man they wanted and forced their way in.
>
> A search uncovered $500,000 in stolen gems.

Sadly, Hugo Wilgerodt remained on the wrong side of the law for the rest of his life. Bertha Willgerodt, the wife of Oscar senior, moved back to NYC and spent the rest of her life in a small one-bedroom apartment in the Washington Heights section of Manhattan, less than 2 miles from her former spacious home on Ogden Avenue. As for little Oscar, he was killed by a train in an accident on Long Island when he was 24.

## Associated Press, Name Card Index to AP Stories

WILLGERODT, Hugo      Englewood, N.J.

Waived extradition after his arrest last night in Englewood, NJ, and is brought to New York after three year search; held for grand larceny; police say is wanted for theft of $24,000 worth of jewels from late Gertrude Williams, one-time Follies girl who committed suicide recently in a furnished room, and also theft of $17,500 worth of jewels from Mrs Margery Ardell      4-25-34 NL14-15 ~~DL24-2-25½~~
Acting Police Capt Patrick McVeigh announces that Willgerodt had admitted taking part in/the two jewelry robberies, and that he said he received only $400 of the $42,000, and named James Brady and Arthur

WILLGERODT, Hugo 2

Rose, who are serving Sing Sing sentences for the Ardell robbery, as accomplices, and that for last three years had been going straight
     4-26-34 DL6
Pleads not guilty in general sessions court
     5-2-34 DL33
Pleads guilty in general sessions court to robbery in third degree while armed; 41 years old; said he took part in the Ardell and Williams robberies
     5-14-34 DL22
Is sentenced to 25 to 30 years in Sing Sing prison by Judge Freschi in general sessions court
     5-21-34 DL9

# *So?*

# What Really Happened

I doubt we will ever learn the true facts about the disappearance of Little Willie McCormick.

In my humble opinion, with more than 60 years of having the missing boy on my mind, and with more than ten years of in-depth research, here's what I'll share.

I became so immersed in Willie's disappearance that I started having dreams about the missing child. In some of these dreams over the past ten years, I felt as if Little Willie was trying to tell me something. At first, I found it extremely difficult to remember the details of the dream. In the mornings after a dream, bits and pieces would pop into my mind during the day. Yet, I did not know if these nuggets of information were coming from my subconscious mind or if I was somehow in contact with the spirit of the missing child.

By my second year of researching old newspapers and interviewing people who may have heard or read stories about Little Willie, the contact with the spirit of Little Willie grew stronger. It was as if we were becoming friends. Willie was telling me things in my dreams that seemed like a crystal clear conversation with a real person. In my subconscious mind, we were becoming friends. Willie was beginning to trust me and I was starting to trust my dreams.

In my dreams, I could tell Willie was still scared of something or someone. The sense of Willie's fear came over me during quite a few of my nightly encounters with him.

It took me another year or so before I realized that Willie was trying to tell me his side of the story—the little insignificant things that were never brought up while the world searched for him.

Eventually, the nightly encounters with the entity, I believe to this day, was his living spirit who somehow found a way to come to me in my dreams and began to tell me more and more about the night he vanished.

One thing I noticed in my dreams, that bothered me in my waking hours, was that Willie wanted me to know how sorry he was for doing some of the stupid things he did while in his earthly shell of William McCormick Junior.

After a few years of dealing with Willie in my dreams, the experience started me down another road. I began doing research and reading books about the paranormal experiences of others who may have, or have claimed, to have had contact with a spirit in their dreams.

The information I garnered by increasing my knowledge about the paranormal and psychic adventures of other earthy beings like myself, opened my mind to a whole new world. I soon became more and more inquisitive and comfortable every time Willie visited.

I did not always keep a diary of these dream events, and for that, I still kick myself in the butt.

To the best of my knowledge, it was about five years ago when the flood gates opened.

I went to bed and I do remember I was very tired. I don't know if you or anyone else reading this had ever had the experience of knowing in your dream that you were actually sleeping and having a dream?

The dream I had that night was a special kind of dream. A type of dream that I had never before experienced. I found myself sitting in a crowded movie theater watching a silent black and white movie flicker across an enormous screen. It was not the size of a screen you's see in a normal modern-day movie house. The dimensions were all off. It must have been as tall as a five-story apartment building and as wide as five regular Movie screens in a large theater.

I remember how strange everything was in that particular dream. As I mentioned, I knew in my dream that I was dreaming. I also knew this dream was being orchestrated by Little Willie McCormick. Another weird thing I experienced in that dream; I remember thinking in my dream—"Willie had died in 1901 and when Willie was alive there were no movies. So, how can this dream be a dream from Willie?" I also remember thinking in this pivotal dream, something is wrong—"Dream-state anachronisms are not allowed in dreams".

Eventually, in my dream, I calmed down and began watching the silent black and white film with the others in the crowded theater.

Suddenly, a dull hum filled the air and everyone in the theater became as quiet as if they were not even there.

The film began with a young boy, who I was 100% sure was Little Willie, bounding down the front steps of a nice house, two and sometimes three steps at a time.

What Really Happened                                              Pat Fogarty

When the boy reached the bottom of the steps he turned left and began running to catch up with some girls who I already knew in my dream were two of his older sisters. At that point in the dream-film, the girls were about a block ahead of him. On the other side of the street, I could see a young man, halfway between Willie and the girls. He was crossing Ogden Avenue at a brisk pace. I watched the film as Little Willie noted the young man and stopped dead in his tracks. For a split second, my mind connected with Little Willie's thoughts and I knew the boy was thinking he could get past this guy and catch up to his sisters before the guy could grab him or do him any harm. That split second of hesitation told Willie and me, still inside his thoughts in the dream, that he should turn and run the other way. And that is exactly what the film showed next. It showed Willie running south on Ogden Avenue in the opposite direction of his sisters and the church he was supposed to be going to.

As the dream film proceeds, I and the other movie-goers in the dream, watch as Willie spots another young man, who he now thinks he recognizes as one of the two guys who chased him home from school the previous week.

At this time in the film, Willie is standing on the southeast corner of Ogden Avenue and 162nd Street. Across Ogden Avenue on the southwest corner of 162nd street stands Mr. Willgerodt. For a moment, Willie's mind is back in my thoughts. My mind and his mind connect once again. Willie is deciding if he wants to cross Ogden Avenue and ask Mr. Willgerodt for help. Willie quickly drops that idea when he remembers how many times he picked on Mr. Willgerodt's son. He also recalls the times when Mr. Reicher, the coachman for the Willgerodt family, told him to stay away from little Oscar, or else!

The flickering film now focuses on the two guys stalking Willie. The young men are now just one block away and talking with each other in front of a Protestant Church on 163rd street. Willie is now sure they are the same two guys he saw a few weeks earlier talking to the old Italian worker he teased every day before going to school. Willie was now more frightened than he had ever been in his entire life.

Without warning, the film jerked to a scene two blocks east to 162nd Street and Anderson Avenue.

In the dream, I knew before the film went any further, exactly what Willie planned to do next. Willie knew he out-ran these two tough-looking guys the week before, so he made up his mind to sprint over to Anderson Avenue and run as fast as he could the six blocks north to the Church where he knew Father Mullin and his sisters would help him. The next image on the screen shows little Willie panting and out of breath standing and fidgeting 50 yards away from the Church. Willie in the dream-film is at the intersection of Anderson Avenue and Marcher Avenue. And as he looks toward the church, he notices the taller of his two stalkers standing in front of the entryway of the church. The lone stalker is grinning and the grin scares him even more. In my dream, I could feel the tenseness of the entire group of my dream movie-goers. It was as if everyone in the crowd was mesmerized by the action on the screen.

The next flicker of the film shows Willie running down Marcher Avenue to Jerome Avenue and continuing at a fast clip south towards the bottom of Ogden Avenue where he knows the backstreets that will get him safely back to his home. There are no streets intersecting Jerome from the West side of the avenue, the natural incline of the terrain is too steep for a street, and on the east side of the deserted Jerome Avenue is the Cromwell Creek and swamp.

The next part of my dream film scares the heck out of me.

Three more rough-looking characters spring from the side of the road and grab Willie. Willie is hysterical. He's crying and calling for help. But this is a deserted and undeveloped area where he could cry all he wanted and no one would hear him. The next part of the film shows the two original stalkers calmly walking south on Jerome Avenue toward the group who were, by then, pushing Willie around.

When the taller stalker finally confronts Willie, he simply grabs Willie's cherished cap from his head and tosses it to one of the three guys who captured the fleeing Willie. For the next few minutes of the film, the five young men continue to toss Willie's cap to each other while Willie cries and tries to get his cap back.

Finally, when the taller stalker, who is obviously the leader of the pack, thinks they've taught little Willie a lesson, he takes Willie's cap, walks over to the edge of the creek, turns, and shouts towards the crying boy; "No more games. You hear me? *Non piu!*"

And then in the dream, the *Leader of the Pack* throws the boy's cap as far as he could into the swamp.

The final scene in my dream shows the five young men walking away from Willie, who is sitting on the ground, holding his head in his hands, and crying.

## Name Changes

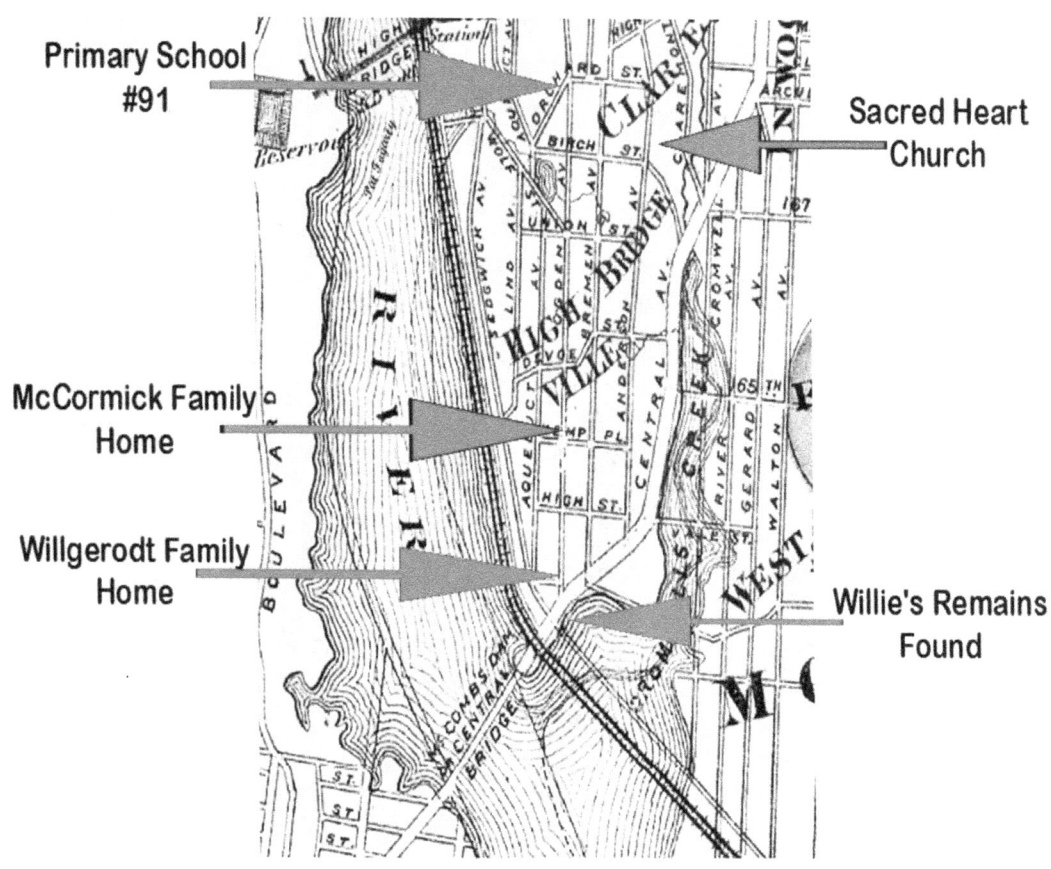

Central Avenue became Jerome Avenue
Kemp Place became 164th Street. High Street became 162nd Street.
Birch Street *on this map* became 168th Street. The extension of *Birch Street* to Central Avenue became Marcher Avenue, which is now named Shakespeare Avenue.
Primary School # 91 on this map was renamed Public School #11
Plus, many of the Street names changed again in later years. Orchard Street is missing. Birch Street should be one block north of its location on the map and in its place should be Orchard Street. The inaccuracy of the older maps would not be noticed by anyone, except maybe by a former resident of Highbridge.

# The Author

Pat Fogarty is an editor, award-winning author, and poet. Born and raised in the South Bronx, his works are infused with personal experiences and historical research. Pat writes Creative Non-fiction, Historical fiction, and literary fiction. Pat also writes short stories and poems which have been published in a plethora of magazines and journals—locally, nationally, and internationally. His short stories have also been included in several anthologies. Pat is the Editor & Publisher of the AZ Writers Best Short Stories, Best Poems, Best New Short Stories, & Best New Poetry series. Pat retired from the International Brotherhood of Electrical Workers in 2005 after 35 years of service. He is also an accredited Alcohol and Substance Abuse Counselor, as well as a Certified Union Counselor. He is currently the President of *The Central Arizona Writers* and past president of the *Professional Writers of Prescott*. Pat is happily married to his soulmate Susan, and together they enjoy spending time at their home in the Mountains of Central Arizona with their German Shepherd and three Irish Terriers.

www.ingramcontent.com/pod-product-compliance
Lightning Source LLC
Chambersburg PA
CBHW081743100526
44592CB00015B/2275